Living by the Spirit

Living by the Spirit

Statements on the Holy Ghost
by Brigham Young
and other early Church leaders

Selected and arranged by

John D. Whetten

Bookcraft
Salt Lake City, Utah

Library of Congress Catalog Card Number: 79-56175
ISBN 0-88494-398-4

4 5 6 7 8 9 10   89 88 87 86 85 84

Lithographed in the United States of America
PUBLISHERS PRESS
Salt Lake City, Utah

To my sweetheart Becky,
whose example of living by the Spirit
has inspired, strengthened and sustained our family

Contents

Preface

While I was attending a graduate research Institute class in the winter of 1967, our teacher gave us an assignment to study a topic from the *Journal of Discourses*. I chose "Living by the Spirit," as I was anxious to know what these early apostles and prophets had learned on the subject.

This initial class assignment that reported on about six speeches by the early Brethren whetted my appetite. During the following years, I compiled and indexed all the references (over 250) contained in the *Journal of Discourses* on this subject.

This research was originally anticipated to be in two parts: the compilation of Living by the Spirit from the *Journal of Discourses* and from the general conference talks of the apostles and prophets since 1900, with special emphasis on the current prophets. This book, however, contains only material from the *Journal of Discourses,* the reference from that source being supplied for each excerpt.

In each of our lives there are moments of stress and strain, trial and tribulation. I have frequently been strengthened during such times by reading the scriptures and from working on this compilation. Peace, insights, and greater determination have come from reading of these early Brethren's faith and reliance on the Lord. They lived by the Spirit of the Lord. They were acquainted with how the Holy Ghost directed them and what they had to do to continue to receive that inspiration.

As this compilation is a reference book, quotations are sometimes used in more than one place. In most cases, the punctuation and spelling have been left as recorded. However, since some original paragraphs are very lengthy, I have divided such paragraphs to make it easier to read.

I am especially grateful for the influence of my parents, Lester and Kate Whetten, who taught me to seek inspiration in the big and little matters of life; and for my wife, Becky Pearse Whetten, whose gifts of intuition and inspiration have often guided and encouraged our family. This book would not have been possible without the encouragement, support, and hours of proofreading given by Becky.

1

The Holy Ghost

A Member of the Godhead

The Holy Ghost, we believe, is one of the characters that form the Trinity, or the Godhead. Not one person in three, nor three persons in one; but the Father, Son, and the Holy Ghost are one in essence, as the hearts of three men who are united in all things. He is one of the three characters we believe in, whose office it is to administer to those of the human family who love the truth.

I have stated that they are one, as the hearts of three men might be one. Lest you should mistake me, I will say that I do not wish you to understand that the Holy Ghost is a personage having a tabernacle, like the Father and the Son; but he is God's messenger that diffuses his influence through all the works of the Almighty.

Brigham Young 6:95

The Holy Ghost is the Spirit of the Lord, and issues forth from Himself, and may properly be called God's minister to execute His will in immensity; being called to govern by His influence and power; but He is not a person of tabernacle as we are, and as our Father in Heaven and Jesus Christ are.

Brigham Young 1:50
See also 2:338; 3:104; 4:362; 15:231, 232

Attributes of the Holy Ghost

A.   Does Not Deceive

Our eyes and ears may be deceived by the cunning and machinations of man; but the Holy Ghost never deceives anybody. It bears record of the Father and the Son, and it bears record in the Gospel to those who possess it.

Wilford Woodruff 19:360

When a man receives the Holy Ghost he has a testimony that can not deceive him or anybody else. . . . but get the Holy Ghost and you have a testimony that can not deceive you. It never deceived any man, and it never will.

Wilford Woodruff 16:38

The sight of the eye, the hearing of the ear, the touch of the hand may each and all be deceived, but the instructions of the spirit are in all things correct. The combined senses may misguide or fail, but he who happily secures the companionship of the Holy Spirit, walks in the ways of life and neither fears, becomes weary nor faints by the wayside.

Moses Thatcher 23:196

B.   Will Not Fail Men

To know and to worship the true God, in the name of Jesus — in spirit and in truth — is the duty of man. To aid and qualify him for this service is the duty and office of the Holy Ghost. Man may fail through faltering and unfaithfulness, but the Spirit of God will never fail, nor abandon the faithful disciple.

Joseph F. Smith 19:191

C.   Is the Same Today as Yesterday

The same Holy Ghost has rested down upon them as rested down upon the Saints in ancient times, and has produced the very same results. For the Holy Ghost has not changed, God has not changed, the truth has not changed, and the Lord is just as willing today as He was in the first years of the Christian era to reveal himself to those who desire to learn of Him, and the Holy Ghost is just as much a revealer today as it was in the olden times when the Prophets wrote and spoke under its influence.

Charles W. Penrose 25:47
See also 20:216-217

D.   Is Omnipresent

We heard a most excellent discourse last Sunday about the angels being sent to the various nations of the earth, to superintend the affairs and destinies thereof; also about each person upon the face of the whole earth having his guardian angel from the time that he comes into the world.

The Holy Spirit acts in conjunction with those angels, and in places where they cannot be, for there are a great many places where those angels cannot be present, and the Holy Spirit being omnipresent is in every place at the same moment of time, regulating the seasons, and governing the planets in their courses. . . .

The Holy Spirit "is in all things, and round about all things," holding all things together in every place and part of the earth, and in all the vast creations of the Almighty. If you ascend into heaven, it is there: if you take the wings of the morning and fly to the uttermost parts of the earth, it is there. . . .

Go where you will, through endless space, and you will find the Spirit there, and consequently, when we speak of the omnipresence of God, we have reference to His Spirit, and not to His person. But why is this called the omnipresence of God? Simply because this Spirit possesses the same knowledge that dwells in the persons of God the Father and God the Son, hence God is there, so far as that knowledge is there.

> Orson Pratt 2:343, 344
> See also 2:339-340

E. Is in Unity with the Father and Son

Now, ask yourselves whether you believe that the Holy Ghost ever commenced to produce a work or an effect before it was in the heart and mind of that Being we call our heavenly Father. Do you think that the Holy Ghost ever thought of dictating that Being we call our God? This whole people have learned enough upon this subject to answer at once, that we do not believe that the Holy Ghost ever dictated, suggested, moved, or pretended to offer a plan, except that which the Eternal Father dictated. . . .

Have we not learned enough with regard to the character of the Father, Son, and Holy Ghost, to at once believe, admit, and affirm that the Holy Ghost always has and always will operate precisely according to the suggestion of the Father? Not a desire, act, wish, or thought does the Holy Ghost indulge in contrary to that which is dictated by the Father.

> Brigham Young 6:95

The Purpose of the Holy Ghost

The office of the Holy Spirit is to enlighten the minds of the people with regard to the things of God, to convince them at the time of their conversion of their having done the will of the Father, and to be in them an abiding testimony as a companion through life, acting as the sure and safe guide into all truth and filling them day by day with joy and gladness, with a disposition to do good to all men, to suffer wrong rather than to do wrong, to be kind and merciful, long suffering and charitable. All who possess this inestimable gift, this pearl of great price, have a continual thirst after righteousness.

> Without the aid of the Holy Spirit no mortal can walk in the straight and narrow way, being unable to discern right from wrong, the genuine from the counterfeit, so nearly alike can they be made to appear. Therefore it behooves the Latter-day Saints to live pure and upright, in order that this Spirit may abide in them; for it is only possessed on the principle of righteousness.

> Joseph F. Smith 18:275

If the all-wise Spirit gains an existence in man, it endeavors to influence and persuade him to become one with God, as it is one with Him.

> Orson Pratt 2:341
> See 2:338-341 for influence of the Holy Ghost on the laws of nature

The Mission of the Holy Ghost

A.   Administers to the Human Family

He [the Holy Ghost] is one of the three characters we believe in, whose office it is to administer to those of the human family who love the truth. . . . He is God's messenger that diffuses his influence through all the works of the Almighty.

> Brigham Young 6:95

The Holy Ghost is God's minister, and is delegated to visit the sons and daughters of men. All intelligent beings pertaining to this earth are instructed from the same source (the Holy Ghost).

> Brigham Young 9:254

B.   Directs the Priesthood

The Seventies were spoken to and counseled to pursue a certain course a few days ago, but did they do it? No they did not. It is not the Seventies that speak, it is not the High Priests, neither is it the Twelve, nor Brigham Young, but it is the Holy Ghost through those various channels that is calling upon the people to carry out the mind and will of our Father who is in heaven.

It is God that is all in all, Him whom we call our Father in heaven,

He qualifies us upon the earth, and we speak forth by the dictation of His Spirit the things that are necessary to be laid before the people.
Lorenzo Snow 4:159

When we go forth as the servants of God, we are dictated by the Holy Ghost, and the Holy Ghost will speak the truth, and that is the word of God, it is the revelations of Jesus Christ, and it is the voice of God to us.
Heber C. Kimball 2:221

C.   Reveals Things of the Godhead

The Holy Ghost is then the special gift of the Father, and is his minister. He also gives intelligence by angels, as well as by the inspiration of the Holy Spirit, and by opening the minds of the Saints to behold in vision things as they are in eternity.
Brigham Young 9:254

We have been made partakers, in a measure, of the spirit of the living God, pertaining to this last dispensation. This spirit, when received, and when we give it our attention, and bring our minds to bear upon the object of its operations, is calculated to instruct and impart much information and knowledge to both male and female who are in the possession of it. The Spirit of God is a spirit of revelation. It always was a spirit that revealed something to the human family, when mankind were in possession of it.
Orson Pratt 21:256

It takes of the things of the Father and makes them plain to the human mind; it makes things past clear to the understanding of man, and it lifts up the curtain of futurity and shows things to come.
Charles W. Penrose 20:217
See also 23:197, 350

D.   Testifies to the Truth

Is there a conviction upon the minds of the people, when they have heard the Gospel preached, and where they have heard of it? Is there a conviction conveyed by the Holy Spirit that this is the Gospel of salvation? There is; and it cannot be denied without falsifying the truth.
Brigham Young 8:131

E.   Is the Seal of Authority

No man has authority to preach the Gospel and administer its ordinances without a commission from Jesus Christ; and the seal of such commission has always been, and always will be the gifts, blessings and endorsement of the Holy Ghost, which not only leads to the form, but also to the power of godliness.

Moses Thatcher 23:197

2

Light of Christ

Given to All Men

We are told, that "there is a spirit in man and the inspiration of the Almighty giveth them understanding." This is that spirit. It is the light of Christ; it is the light of God. It is the life of our bodies, and it is also the light of our minds.

This spirit is not confined to one race of people, or to one country, or to one age or generation, but it is universal; it is of Him in whom we live and move and have our being. It is the true light that lighteth every man that cometh into the world. And if all men would be guided by that natural light, that natual inspiration which gives them understanding, and by which they exist, they would be guided directly to Him who is the fountain of all light; they would then be in a condition to be communicated with by Him who is their Maker and Creator.

Charles W. Penrose 23:346-347
See also 2:138-140; 22:85; 23:346

Knowledge/Inventions Come from Light of Christ

And furthermore, whatever correct religious ideas that the world possess in relation to the future state, proceed from that portion of the Spirit that is given to every man to profit withal — not unto us only, but to every man, and to the influence of that Spirit all men are indebted for the degree of honor and integrity that exists among men. It is true that is very little comparatively, but for the amount there is they are indebted to God just as much as we are.

John Taylor 20:222

All valuable inventions and works of mechanism are produced by a Spirit that flows from the Fountain of intelligence, and no excellent and magnanimous work can be produced without that Spirit.
        Brigham Young 7:158

There are men of talent, of thought, of reflection, and knowledge in all cunning mechanism: they are expert in that, though they do not know from whence they receive their intelligence. The Spirit of the Lord has not yet entirely done striving with the people, offering them knowledge and intelligence; consequently it reveals unto them, instructs them, teaches them and guides them even in the way they like to travel.

Men know how to construct railroads and all manner of machinery; they understand cunning workmanship, etc.; but that is all revealed to them by the Spirit of the Lord though they know it not.
        Brigham Young 5:124-125
        See also 10:216; 23:247

Strives with People to Do Right

How does the child, or youth, immediately know when he performs the first wicked act of his life? Is there not within him a consciousness of right and wrong? This is a portion of the divinity which lights every one who is born into the world, which acts as a monitor to the heart and soul, and never fails to impress the mind with an unmistakable sense of right and wrong.
        Joseph F. Smith 18:276

Are they [other Christians] entitled to that degree of the Spirit of God that we are? No, but they are entitled to light. And there is one saying I heard here today, that I will repeat; whenever any one lifts his voice or hand to persecute this people, there is a chill passes through him, unless he is lost to truth and the Spirit of God has entirely left him.

He feels it day and night; he feels the Spirit working with him. And the Spirit of the Lord will strive, and strive, and strive with the people, till they have sinned away the day of grace. Until then, all are entitled to the light of Christ, for he is the light that lighteth every man who cometh into the world.
        Brigham Young 10:296

He [Satan] has power over us to that extent [to tempt us] in this fallen condition. At the same time we have the sweet influence of the Spirit of God pleading with us to do that which is right, pleading with every human being that does not drive it from him; for every human being has a portion of the Spirit of God given unto him.

We sometimes call it conscience; we call it by one name and we call it by another; but it is the Spirit of God that every man and woman possesses that is born on the earth. God has given unto all his children this Spirit. Of course it is not the gift of the Holy Ghost in its fullness; for that is only received by obedience to the commandments of God — to the Gospel of our Lord and Savior Jesus Christ.

Everywhere throughout the earth where man dwells this Spirit rests upon him. It comes from God. It pleads with man to do right. It pleads with man to resist the blandishments of Satan. No man ever did a wrong but that Spirit warned him of it to a greater or less extent. No man ever put his hand forth to do a wrong to his neighbor without that Spirit telling him it was wrong. He never put forth his hand or influence to wrong the gentler sex — to commit sin in that direction — without that warning voice which is in every human being telling him of the sin.

George Q. Cannon 26:191

Will Lead You to God and to More Light

He lighteth every man that cometh into the world. This is the same spirit which is called the Comforter, although it does not operate in the same degree as that spirit which is called the gift of the Holy Ghost, which we read about in the New Testament, in the promises of Jesus Christ to his disciples and to those who would keep his commandments; but all people born into the world receive a portion of divine light, and if they would grow up under the influence of that light and be actuated and guided by its whisperings all through their earthly career, it would lead them gradually up to the fountain of light, to "the Father of lights, with whom is no variableness, neither shadow of turning."

It would lead gradually to God, so that they could commune with God while they remain in the flesh; they would grow up nearer and nearer to Him, for they would choose the good and refuse the evil; they would take into their nature that which would lead them towards God, and they would repel from them that which would lead downward, they would discern the strait and narrow path that leadeth unto life, and they would avoid the broad road which leadeth unto destruction, in which so many of the human family have walked from the beginning. It is because the people that dwell on the earth do not listen to the "still small voice" of that natural light which is born with them into the world, that they do not receive the things of God.

Charles W. Penrose 22:85

The Difference Between the Light of Christ and the Gift of the Holy Ghost

There is and always has been a spirit abroad in the world which is really a portion of the Spirit of God, which leads mankind, in many instances, to discriminate between good and evil, and between right and wrong. They have a conscience that accuses or excuses them for their acts; and although the world of mankind is very wicked and very corrupt, yet it will be found that almost all men, though they may not do good themselves, appreciate good actions in others. . . .

The Scripture further says, He has given unto them a portion of his spirit to profit withal. But there is quite a distinction between the position that these people occupy and the one which we occupy. We have something more than that portion of the Spirit of God which is given to every man, and it is called the gift of the Holy Ghost, which is received through obedience to the first principles of the Gospel of Christ, by the laying on of hands of the servants of God. . . .

They [the early Christians] were told, moreover, what this Holy Ghost would do; that it would take of the things of God and shew them unto them; that it would cause their old men to dream dreams and their young men to see visions; and that it would rest upon the servants and handmaids of God, and they should prophesy.

These are the operations of that Spirit which dwells with God, the Father, and God, the Son, namely the Holy Ghost. It is this Spirit that brings us into relationship with God, and it differs very materially from the portion of spirit that is given to all men to profit withal. The special gift of the Holy Ghost is obtained, as I have said, through obedience to the first principles of the Gospel. Its province is to lead us into all truth, and to bring to our remembrance things past, present and to come. It contemplates the future and unfolds things we had not thought of heretofore. . . . Herein lies the difference between us and others, and it was so in former times.

> John Taylor 23:320-321
> See also 14:304; 23:374; 25:212

3

The Gift
of the Holy Ghost

In using that term, the "gift of the Holy Ghost," we do not mean some particular gift of the Spirit, but the gift of the Spirit itself — the Holy Ghost given unto us as a gift from God. . . .

The promise is to those who will repent and be baptized for the remission of sins; they shall receive "the gift of the Holy Ghost." What is it?

It is a greater and higher endowment of the same spirit which enlightens every man that comes into the world; a greater power given unto us as an abiding witness, to be a light to our feet and a lamp to our path; as a restraint against sin, to guide us into all truth, to open up the vision of the mind, to bring things past to our remembrance, and to make manifest things to come. It is the spirit of truth that reveals the things of the Father and the Son, proceeding from the presence of the Almighty and the very glory in which He is enrobed, which makes him like unto a consuming fire.

If we receive that heavenly gift all are brought into communion with Him; we can understand something concerning Him, that we may pattern after Him until we become like Him; for if we are continually guided by that spirit, eventually we will come back to His presence and be able to enjoy the fullness of His glory. And while we remain in the flesh He will not be a stranger to us; we will not walk in the dark like the majority of mankind, but we will be the children of the light, comprehending the truth as it is in Him, and seeing the path in which we should walk.

Charles W. Penrose 23:350

Wherever the servants of God have gone bearing this message, and the people have received it and obeyed the requirements of the Gospel, they have received the Holy Ghost as a gift from on high; and if they have been led by its light it has increased in them day by day, and they are still going on, their light growing brighter and brighter unto the perfect day.

Charles W. Penrose 23:352

The hands of the servants of God were laid upon my head, and I received the Holy Ghost — that same Spirit which God gave to the prophets, that same Spirit which rested upon John upon the Isle of Patmos, that same Spirit by which holy men of old wrote and spoke as they were moved upon by the Holy Ghost; and that Spirit is the same yesterday, today and forever.

It takes of the things of the Father and makes them plain to the human mind; it makes things past clear to the understanding of man, and it lifts up the curtain of futurity and shows things to come. It is the spirit of prophecy, the testimony of Jesus; it is the light of God to the human soul. And as natural light discloses to the vision of men the objects of the material universe, without which none can discern them, so the Holy Ghost is the light of God which reveals to the spirits of men the things of eternal life, and without which men cannot understand the things of God.

It is because of the absence of this divine light that the world lies in darkness in regard to their Father and God; this is why men, notwithstanding their learning, their scientific discoveries in the material universe, cannot comprehend the things of God. Man by searching cannot find out God. He can reveal himself to mankind, but must do it through the Son, and obedience to the Gospel of his Son is the only way of salvation. There is no other, and no name given under heaven whereby man can be saved but the name of Jesus Christ.

Charles W. Penrose 20:216-217

Then we have the great privilege given us of God, that all the time we may draw near unto the throne of grace and receive for ourselves, individually as well as collectively, the power of the Holy Spirit to enlighten us in regard to the purposes of God, to strengthen us against sin, to enable us to cultivate the good that is in us, and grow up unto Him who is our living head in all things, even the Lord Jesus.

This is the greatest boon that could be conferred upon mortals while dwelling in the flesh, the gift of the Holy Ghost, the Comforter, the spirit of truth, which reveals unto men the things of the Father and of the Son, which is a spiritual light to the inward being, which is the same to the spiritual nature of man as the light that streams from the sun to the physical nature of man.

As we are able to see the various physical objects of creation by the light of the sun, or as we call it, natural light, so by the aid of this spiritual light we can discern the things of God, and they can be made just as plain to our spiritual eyesight by the power of the Holy Spirit, as the things of the earth are made plain to our natural eyes by the power of the natural light that comes from the sun, or any artificial means which they may use or discover.

Charles W. Penrose 22:84-85

How Given

The Holy Ghost, this greater endowment of that spirit which naturally enlighteneth every man that comes into the world, is conferred upon us through a simple process, the way that God has ordained; and it can come in no other way.

If there should be any in this congregation this afternoon who desire to know God, or if they desire to know themselves, they must take this one course — they can do as they please about it, either to receive or reject it, but if they want the blessing of it, they must seek for it in His way. They cannot get it through manmade systems; God has His own way. He acknowledges not, neither does He recognize the ways of men; but if people will hearken to Him and walk in His ways He will be nigh unto them, and will bear testimony to them in language that they, by the power and gift of His spirit can understand.

But they must believe; they must also repent; and that repentance that is necessary does not consist in weeping and mourning over sin, but in turning away from it. No man can make God his friend by continuing in sin, neither can any woman. In order to come near unto God and to be taught of Him, they must be humble and child-like, they must be willing to receive instruction, being determined in their hearts to turn away from wrong-doing of every kind, and to cleave unto that which is right.

Charles W. Penrose 23:352
See also 9:254

Given to Whom

God bestows his Holy Spirit upon those who obey his Gospel as he bestows light upon the earth. There have not been a privileged few, there has been no hierarchy, there has been no monopoly of knowledge, for some exclusive set to receive while the rest would be destitute; but it has been diffused like the blessing of air — it has been to all who have believed it, and every man and woman has received a testimony for himself and herself respecting the Gospel of Jesus Christ as it has been revealed and taught in these last days.

      George Q. Cannon 16:243

Every man and every woman and every child who have come to years of accountability can receive direct from the Lord, direct from the fountain of their being, a testimony by which they may know that he lives, that they are walking in his ways, and learn how they can approach him acceptably.

      Charles W. Penrose 20:217

I cannot receive it for you, nor you for me; every one must stand for him or her self, whether of high or humble birth, learned or unlearned, and it is the privilege of all alike to be made partakers of it.

      Joseph F. Smith 18:275
      See also 4:4-5; 10:321; 14:178; 24:129; 25:47

Why Given

The gift and power of the Holy Ghost, as I have already observed, is the greatest evidence any man or woman can have concerning the kingdom of God. It is given expressly to impart to mankind a knowledge of the things of God. It is given to purify the heart of man, that he may by its power not only be able to understand its operations upon himself, but be able to understand its operations upon others also.

      Orson Pratt 7:179

4

How the
Holy Ghost Guides You

Will Tell You in Your Mind, Spirit and Heart

My reason for calling your attention to the word of the Lord I have read to you is, that I have sometimes thought that our people do not appreciate as they should do the spirit of revelation, the spirit of prophecy, the power of God, that has been poured out upon us as a people.

The fact seems to be overlooked that it was in [this] manner in which the Lord tells Oliver Cowdery that Moses brought the children of Israel through the Red Sea on dry ground. The Lord said to Oliver: "I will tell you in your mind and in your heart, by the Holy Ghost, which shall come upon you, and which shall dwell in your heart. Now, behold, this is the spirit of revelation; behold, this is the spirit by which Moses brought the children of Israel through the Red Sea on dry ground".....

How many are there at the present time who are neglecting the precious and inestimable gift of revelation which God has bestowed upon his people, because it does not come to them in the way to suit their preconceived notions and ideas — or who are not suited with the way the Church has been and is led, because there is not that wonderful degree of power exhibited which they imagine should be?

George Q. Cannon 21:268

There is not a truth extant upon the earth today that has been utilized, or many truths combined together that have been utilized but have been the result of divine inspiration directly to the spirit of man, to the mind of man which is sometimes incorrectly called the soul of Man.

Joseph E. Taylor 23:247

How You Feel When Guided by the Holy Ghost

I have no doubt that there are many others among the people of God, who can see where they have erred, because they did not have the Spirit of God upon them at the time.

I can see, also, many times when the Spirit of the Lord whispered to me, and I scarcely knew whether it was my own thoughts and imaginations or whether it was the revelations of the Spirit; yet it seemed to be the Spirit of the Lord, and I followed the teachings, and was prospered in so doing.

The idea is that in these tabernacles of ours we have an intelligent spirit which God has placed there, and he has ordained that the Spirit of the Lord shall light up these human spirits of ours, that we may follow in the paths of light, truth and righteousness and obtain eternal life.

Orson Pratt 15:230

And when hands were laid upon me by the servants of God, and I received the gift of the Holy Ghost, I felt no physical manifestation. I must say, I felt a little disappointed at first, for I had expected some such manifestation, but I did not receive any at that time. What did I experience? I found that my mind was opened, that I had greater light; that something had come upon me by which I could see clearly the things of God; and when I read the scriptures new light dawned upon them.

I was brought up to believe in the Bible. I had read it when a child, and committed a great deal of it to memory; and when I received this gift from the Almighty through the laying on of hands, it brought those things that were past to my remembrance; they stood up clearly and in bold relief before me, and I could comprehend something concerning God. I could feel that I was in communion with Him. When I prayed I could realize that my words were heard, that God hearkened and answered. When I prayed for knowledge and understanding concerning the things of God, they were manifested to me.

It brought to me that which is called in the Scriptures, "the peace of God that passeth all understanding." The joy, the peace, the satisfaction that it brought to me could not be described in words. I knew that my Redeemer lived; I knew that I was born again; I knew the Holy Spirit was working in my heart. Truths were manifested to me that I had never heard of or read of, but which I afterwards heard preached by the servants of the Lord; all this was testimony to me that I had received the truth.

Charles W. Penrose 23:351

When the brethren are traveling and preaching, they have the spirit of obedience; and while we are here preaching to you the Spirit of the Lord broods over the congregation, your countenances are lit up with heavenly intelligence, your hearts are one, and you are ready to observe every word of counsel that is given to you, and each and every one feels to say, "It is my delight to do the will of God."

Brigham Young 10:310

Will Not Force You

When men choose to receive the light of truth, the spirit of truth prompts them to do good, but it does not force them to do so; it is gentle and kind, and will enlighten and bless if people are willing to receive and act upon its promptings; but if men choose to walk in their own ways, they are at liberty to do so without let or hindrance, so far as the spirit of light forcing itself upon them to compel them to walk in the way of the Lord, is concerned.

Charles W. Penrose 23:347

5

Living for
the Holy Ghost

Live a Righteous Life

Without the aid of the Holy Spirit no mortal can walk in the straight and narrow way, being unable to discern right from wrong, the genuine from the counterfeit, so nearly alike can they be made to appear. Therefore it behooves the Latter-day Saints to live pure and upright, in order that this Spirit may abide in them; for it is only possessed on the principle of righteousness. I cannot receive it for you, nor you for me; every one must stand for him or her self, whether of high or humble birth, learned or unlearned, and it is the privilege of all alike to be made partakers of it.

Joseph F. Smith 18:275

We have been seeking, in a great measure, to do the will of our heavenly Father, to keep his commandments, magnify our Priesthood, honour our calling, and do that which is right in the sight of God continually. Inasmuch as we have done this, the Spirit of God is yet with us — a living, abiding, eternal principle, which is extending, growing, and increasing within us, until we shall be prepared to associate with the Gods of eternity.

John Taylor 7:318

We should let the Spirit of the Lord rule, and the law of God abide in our hearts. If we have the law of God dwelling in us, and if we practice righteousness and live by correct principles, we may have it, and will increase in light and in power with the heavens and with all good men. We should cherish that law, let it abide in us, govern and control us in all we do and say. Let us square our ideas, feelings, and spirits to it, and bear in mind that this is what preserves us and connects us together in the strait and narrow way that leads unto life eternal.

> Daniel H. Wells 9:95

And hence the necessity all the day long, and every day, and every week, month, and year, and under all circumstances, of men leaning upon the Lord and being guided by that Spirit that flows from him, that we may not fall into error — that we may neither do anything wrong, say anything wrong, nor think anything wrong, and all the time retain that Spirit, which can only be kept by observing purity, holiness, and virtue, and living continually in obedience to the laws and commandments of God.

> John Taylor 6:106
> See also 6:164; 20:227

Have Peace, Harmony and Word of God in Your Home

You want to live so that your minds will be filled with his Spirit; and to do this, you need not take a mission to the sun, to the moon, or to the stars, to find out their distances or how much they weigh. But are you acquainted with your homes? You answer, "Yes." Well, then, do right at home, do not do wrong, do not quarrel at home, do not stir up disunion, do not, in a word, do anything to bring about a pandemonium instead of a paradise; but do that which brings peace — that which produces the spirit of peace and of heaven.

But where division of sentiment, diversity of feeling, and discord exist, the principles of heaven are not there; the principles of peace are not there. Study these principles, and for what purpose? Why, that it may stir up the spirit of peace within you — that the spirit of peace may be, not a casual visitor, but a constant attendant — that he may take up his abode with you; and when an individual takes up his abode with you, then you do not consider him a transient visitor, but there is his home — there is where he lodges, where he stays, where he imparts blessings — if he is a minister of blessings, where he imparts good, if he has any good to impart.

And if you open a door that this Spirit will take up his abode with you, then that fountain which will be opened up will become very plenteous in its supplies; it will become so to you because you welcome the Holy Spirit there, and you study to cultivate within you such a feeling that the Spirit will love to tarry with you day by day; and its book of instructions will be opened to you, so that each succeeding day will give you an increase of knowledge, and you will find yourselves able to comprehend one degree of light and knowledge after another, until your whole soul will be swallowed up in your love for the truth; your affections will be bound up in the truth, for which you will be willing to sacrifice all; and you will throw away all the old fogyism that was around you; and if you have acted as if you thought the world was yours, then you will think that it is your Father's, and that he only lent it. You will acknowledge his ownership to it, and you will give yourself to him and to his cause continually.

    Amasa M. Lyman 5:310

The men who are sitting here this day ought to be, when in the presence of their families, filled with the Holy Ghost, to administer the word of life to them as it is administered in this stand from sabbath to sabbath. When they kneel down in the presence of their wives and children they ought to be inspired by the gift and power of the Holy Ghost, that the husband may be such a man as a good wife will honor, and that the gift and power of God may be upon them continually.

They ought to be one in their families, that the Holy Ghost might descend upon them, and they ought to live so that the wife through prayer may become sanctified, that she may see the necessity of sanctifying herself in the presence of her husband, and in the presence of her children, that they may be one together, in order that the man and the wife may be pure element, suitable to occupy a place in the establishment and formation of the kingdom of God, that they may breathe a pure spirit and impart pure instruction to their children, and their children's children.

    Lorenzo Snow 4:155

It is the same with every wrong thought and evil suggestion that may occur to your minds. What will be done if you act on this principle? The Father at home, if he thinks a wrong thing won't say it. The wife and mother will do the same; and what will be the result? Harmony in the domestic circle will never be destroyed by evil speaking. What then?

If harmony be there, the Spirit of God will be there. Why? Because it delights to dwell in a quiet place; it does not love contention; it is no friend to strife; it is not fond of bickering or saying hard things. The Spirit of God will come and take his abode with us, if we prepare our minds for its reception, and make it welcome, and study to cultivate a feeling that is congenial with its own nature.

    Amasa M. Lyman 5:39

Have Composure and Order Before the Lord

Brethren and sisters, let your minds be composed and settled down in the Spirit of the Lord, and have his Spirit to be with you always, and especially when you come to the house of worship.
  Heber C. Kimball 7:16

President Kimball: Shut that door and let it remain so, for I tell you there is no one can enjoy the peaceful influence of the Holy Spirit where there is confusion; and I am sure this congregation cannot while that door is going clickitty-clack.

[President Heber C. Kimball interrupted Wilford Woodruff's talk to make the above observation.]
  Heber C. Kimball 4:191
  See also 5:39, the Spirit of God "delights to dwell in a quiet place" (quoted in the previous section)

Obey God's Commandments

We were told that by obedience to that Gospel we should be made the recipients of a Spirit which would bring things past to our remembrance, that would lead us into all truth and show us things to come.

Believing in this message, this vast crowd of people before me today, went forth and bowed in obedience, and they received that Spirit, and they knew and do know that the Gospel they had preached unto them came not in word only, but in power and in the demonstration of the Spirit, and that the Holy Ghost accompanied it.
  John Taylor 13:226-227

Now, if we yield obedience to God and to the spirits that dwell within us, then will our light become like that of the just that shineth brighter and brighter unto the perfect day; but if we do not yield an obedience to the law and word and order of the Church and Kingdom of God upon the earth, the light that is within us will become darkness, and then, as it is said, how great is that darkness!
  John Taylor 26:130-131

Will the Lord bestow his Holy Spirit upon an unwise and unfaithful servant — upon one who disobeys his commandments, who sits himself down in idleness, and will not attempt to inform his mind upon all subjects within his reach? If any person supposes this, he is greatly mistaken; but if he tries to fulfill the commandments of God, making himself extensively acquainted with the attributes of that Being whom he worships — if he tries to become acquainted with all useful subjects, he will then have faith.

Orson Pratt 7:75

That is the office of the Holy Ghost — to dwell and abide with those who keep the commandments of the Almighty in faith believing. He delights to dwell with such; but he does not delight to dwell in unholy temples.

Heber C. Kimball 7:17

It is only by being obedient and submitting to the counsel of God in all things, that we can fully enjoy that good Spirit. By acting upon this principle in a family capacity and in managing our individual concerns (for it is in thus acting upon the principles of obedience that families are united), that Spirit will unite, connect, and cause the Elders to see eye to eye, and thus promote the advancement and prosperity of the cause we have all espoused. We cannot fulfill our engagements with the Almighty without we have that Spirit with us. We should so live as to acknowledge the Good Spirit continually. We cannot do this unless we let the Spirit of God rule in temporalities as well as in spiritual matters.

Daniel H. Wells 9:94-95
See also 24:179

Remove Every Obstacle

If I do not enjoy the Holy Spirit, there is something the matter, and I should labour until that is removed, for I consider that to be the first turning key, and we should do this to prove that we are honest before the Lord, and that we desire to do right in our minds and in our hearts.

Wilford Woodruff 4:191

Many a soul may be drooping for the want of spiritual moisture, and they do not know what the difficulty is. There are obstacles in the way that need removing, that our minds may be enlightened by the light of the Spirit of the living God.

Daniel H. Wells 12:234
See also 18:99-100

Repent/Labor and Be Faithful

He likes to see his children who have repented and obeyed his Gospel joyful and happy, and he is willing to give good gifts unto them; but he never can to those who do not keep his commandments.

They may pray until they are greyheaded and they are about to fall into their graves and their sins would not be pardoned.

Orson Pratt 14:178

You must repent of your evil deeds and first of all morally reform yourselves, before you can ask God for His Spirit to reform and enlighten your spirits.

Brigham Young 4:61

But I know that it requires constant warfare, labor and faithfulness before the Lord in order for us to keep in fellowship with the Holy Spirit, and to live in such a manner that we may obtain these blessings.

Wilford Woodruff 18:35-36

Live Pure Lives

I say, the Holy Ghost, being a pure spirit or influence, even after all this is done [receiving the gift of the Holy Ghost], will have an objection to perform his office in an impure tabernacle. That is the reason why a great many never receive the Holy Ghost, because they say they are pure, and lie to God, and also to the Holy Ghost.

Heber C. Kimball 7:16

We know that it is as strict a law of heaven as any other that has been given, that the man who enters into this Church, and practices impurity, will lose the Spirit of God, and, sooner or later, will be opposed to this Work. . . .

We who are connected with this Church, and retain our membership with this people, must be pure in our thoughts, in our words, and in our actions; we must take a course to retain the Spirit of God in our hearts; and if we do not take a course of this kind, the Spirit of God will inevitably leave us, and that light which has illumined our understandings, that joy and peace which have filled our souls and caused us to rejoice exceedingly before the Lord, will depart from us, and we shall be left in a worse condition than we were before we obeyed the Gospel.

George Q. Cannon 11:226

These bodies are given to you by the same Being that gave to me my body, and they are committed to you as a stewardship by that God who placed us here; and you have got to give an account of your stewardship, and the course you take. If you permit that tabernacle to become polluted, and if your spirit suffers your body to be contaminated with sin and corruption, you will have to make an atonement for it before you can get your redemption worked out. Gentlemen, mark it, for it is even so.

Heber C. Kimball 1:34
See also 4:152-153

Live Clean Lives

The temporal will keep pace as the spiritual advances. I do not believe that a man who is full of the Holy Ghost is going to live contentedly in a hog pen, in filth and in dirt, when it is in his power to prevent it. . . .

If you want the Holy Ghost, keep yourselves clean. I know that some think, when they get here, "O, we are in Zion, everything is right; there is no use in washing our children or combing their hair." I want you to understand that we wish you to be clean outside as well as inside; we want you to be clean and pure; to be good natured and possessed of every qualification requisite in a Saint of God; to have everything that can bring the light and gift of God among you.

Jedediah M. Grant 4:152

That is the office of the Holy Ghost — to dwell and abide with those who keep the commandments of the Almighty in faith believing. He delights to dwell with such; but he does not delight to dwell in unholy temples. You know that naturally, because there is not one of you, unless you make a practice of being filthy and dirty yourselves, that ever wishes to go into a filthy place. Now if these are your feelings, for heaven's sake do not ask the Holy Ghost to dwell with you, when you do not pursue a course to cleanse the body, not only internally, but externally, from the crown of the head to the soles of the feet. You know this is what I believe to be sanctification.

Heber C. Kimball 7:17

Have Balance (Spiritual/Temporal) in Our Lives

We cannot fulfill our engagements with the Almighty without we have that Spirit with us. We should so live as to acknowledge the Good Spirit continually. We cannot do this unless we let the Spirit of God rule in temporalities as well as in spiritual matters.

Daniel H. Wells 9:95

A man that advances in spiritual and in temporal matters at the same time, minding to keep the spiritual first, will not let the temporal lead him; he will not place his heart upon his farm, his horses, or any possession that he has. He will place his desires in heaven, and will anchor his hope in that eternal soil; and his temporal affairs will come up as he advances in the knowledge of God.

Jedediah M. Grant 4:152

Now, I can tell you all candidly that unless you advance in these temporal improvements you never will increase in spiritual knowledge; the one cannot thrive without the other. You may think it strange that you cannot enjoy religion and the Spirit of God in a little, miserable log cabin, but you must remember that the temporal and spiritual go hand in hand, they are inseparably connected, and you may rest assured that the one cannot advance far along the path of progression without the other. This has been one of my principles ever since I came to a knowledge of the truth.

Heber C. Kimball 10:234

We are beginning to understand that there is something, besides that which concerns our spiritual welfare, needed for the upbuilding of the kingdom of God on the earth; we begin to understand that the Lord wishes us to be a people wise in the arts and sciences, full of understanding and wisdom in the building up of cities, in the erection of beautiful habitations and magnificent temples, and in the exhumation of minerals from the bowels of the earth, and their proper application for the beautifying of the cities of Zion and the convenience of God's people. We begin to understand that the Gospel has been revealed to show unto us the object of our existence, that it affects every action of our lives from birth to the grave, and that we cannot do anything but what is comprehended in the Gospel. . . .

There is one point we should be guarded against . . . in our seeking to . . . build up cities and temples and the various works that are incumbent on us, that we should not forget to keep our minds right before the Lord, that we should have his Holy Spirit abiding within us. When the cares of every day life increase upon us, in the business of forming settlements, pioneering and performing our labors from day to day, we are too apt to forget that we should constantly seek to God with the same fervor and diligence for His aid as we do for spiritual blessings.

I find that I have to be careful while engaged in business, for I know that the tendency of my mind is to devote all my thoughts and all my time and attention to the business that is in hand — that happens to occupy my attention at the time. This is the tendency of people generally, and we have to guard against it, and for which we have to be reproved, that we may not yield to it to so great an extent as to drive the Spirit of God from us. There is no necessity for this. If we grieve the

Spirit of God when we are performing our temporal duties, it is because we allow the one idea to absorb our attention too much. While we are engaged in these duties, we should have the Spirit of God resting upon us, as if we were engaged in preaching the Gospel. . . .

I know it requires a struggle to concentrate our thoughts on the things of the Kingdom of God, while we are engaged in business; but this is one of the things which we have to train ourselves to and to overcome.

George Q. Cannon 11:33-34

Have Unity

And on the day of Pentecost, we read, they came together "with one accord in one place." They were of one heart, of one mind, and of one spirit, and then the Holy Ghost was manifested to them, in visible form, in cloven tongues as of fire.

Charles W. Penrose 25:45

They ought to be one in their families, that the Holy Ghost might descend upon them, and they ought to live so that the wife through prayer may become sanctified. . . .

Lorenzo Snow 4:155

Be Positive

I have come to the conclusion that the more I talk about the right and the less I talk about the wrong, and the more I become occupied with the right the less danger I shall be in of becoming occupied by the wrong. This is good for me, and, being good for me, I recommend it to the Saints.

Amasa M. Lyman 10:87

Fulfill Callings (Spiritual/Temporal)

This is a great and important work — one that we do not fully comprehend. When the Spirit of the Lord rests powerfully upon us, we realize it to some extent; but we do not always have that Spirit in such copious measure, and when we are left to ourselves we are weak, frail and liable to err. This shows to us that we should be more faithful than we have ever been, and that day and night, wherever we are and under whatever circumstances we may be placed, in order to enjoy the Spirit of the Gospel we must live to God by observing truth, honoring his law, and ever manifest a vigorous determination to accomplish the work he has assigned us.

Joseph F. Smith 11:309

If a person is not called to sit in the High Council, he may be called to be a Bishop, and if he is through his ward, faithfully looking after the wants of the poor, examining into the conducts of each and every family. . . . he is laboring faithfully in the discharge of his duty, and is entitled to the Spirit of the Lord to sanctify his own heart and to purify himself, just as much as if he were on his knees praying. . . .

No matter what the person is called to do, if it is to build up the Kingdom of God on the earth, if he cheerfully performs the duty, he is entitled to the Spirit of the Lord — the Spirit of Truth — the Holy Ghost; and will most assuredly possess the same. There is a time for preaching, for praying, for sacrament meetings, for labor, and when we are attending to any or all of these, in the season thereof, we are entitled to the purifying influence of the Spirit of God.

If a man is called to go and farm, and he goes faithfully about it, because he is directed to do so by the authorities that are over him, and he raises his grain, his cattle, and brings forth his crops to sustain man and beast, and does this with an eye single to the glory of God and for the building up of his kingdom, he is just as much entitled to the Spirit of the Lord, following his plough, as I am in this pulpit preaching, according to the ministry and calling, and the duties devolving upon him. . . .

Will he have the spirit of teaching and expounding the Scriptures? No, he has the spirit to know how to raise sheep, to procure the wool, to put machinery in operation to make the clothing for the advancement, benefit and building up of the people of God on the earth. And the Spirit of the Lord is here in these labors — farming, merchandizing and in all mechanical business just as much as it is in preaching the Gospel, if men will live for it.

Brigham Young 11:293-294
See also 8:269 (quoted in "Live up to Your Covenants" in this chapter)

Follow Your Church Leaders

Your Bishop is laid down by the master workman as the conductor of the Holy Ghost to you. If you put that conductor out of its place, the connection is broken between you and the fountain of light. If you see a Bishop and his Ward in contention and confusion, you may understand that the pipe or conductor which conveys the light of that people is out of its place. Instead of the Bishop's being wrong, and the people right, or the people wrong, and the Bishop right, they are all wrong: there is little or no right there.

Take any man in this kingdom, and if the people say that they will make him a President or a Bishop, or elect him to fill any other office, and the faith of the people is concentrated to receive light through that officer or pipe laid by the power of the Priesthood from the throne of God, you might as well try to move the heavens as to receive anything wrong through that conductor. No matter whom you elect for an officer, if your faith is concentrated in him through whom to receive the things which he is appointed to administer in, light will come to you.

Let a presiding officer or a Bishop turn away from righteousness, and the Lord Almighty would give him the lockjaw, if he could not stop his mouth in any other way, or send a fit of numb palsy on him, so that he could not act, as sure as the people over whom he presided were right, that they might not be led astray.

Brigham Young 6:99

It is therefore your duty to give heed to those placed over you in authority, and if you do, you will enjoy the Spirit of God to a great extent, even to your hearts' satisfaction. We are called upon to uphold, by our faith, works, and our prayers, those who are over us; we have raised our hands to sustain and uphold them, and will we turn round and find fault with that which we have sanctioned? Can you enjoy the Spirit of God if you do this? No. In order to enjoy that spirit, you must reverence all the members of the Priesthood, no matter who may be in possession of it.

Ezra T. Benson 3:63

Live up to Your Covenants

We can enjoy the true comforts of the Holy Ghost. We should honour our calling and be true to the covenants we have made. If we attend to our duties and walk humbly before the Lord, we shall be satisfied with life and with the manifestations of the goodness of God unto us.

Wilford Woodruff 8:269

If we live according to our covenants we will always enjoy the light of truth, and if we live faithful enough we shall enjoy the blessing of the Holy Ghost to be our constant companion.

Brigham Young 10:289

Be Humble

We must learn to be humble, meek and lowly, or we cannot enjoy the Spirit of the Lord.

Charles C. Rich 19:254

If you could just humble yourselves until your eyes should be enlightened by the Spirit of God, by the spirit of intelligence, you may understand things the world cannot see; and understand that it is the privilege of every person to know the exact situation of the inhabitants of the earth, for themselves. The ancient Apostles saw it; Jesus Christ knew all about it; and the Prophets before them prophesied, and wrote, and preached about what was then upon the earth, what had been, and what would be.

> Brigham Young 3:89
> See also 4:191; 8:176, 269; 20:227

Ask in Mighty Prayer

While paying attention to the prayers of some persons in their family devotions, I sometimes notice that they often stop praying without breaking through the darkness and obtaining the Holy Spirit.

If I found that it was necessary to pray three hours I would keep praying for that length of time, or until I got the Spirit, unless I remembered that I had neglected a special duty, when I would go and attend to that duty; after which I should want to return and pray until I got the Holy Ghost; I would keep praying until I broke the ice and obtained the Holy Ghost.

> Jedediah M. Grant 4:151

It is recorded in the Book of Mormon that when the Nephites were oppressed by the Lamanites, who would not suffer them to pray orally unto God, they prayed in their hearts, while engaged in their labors, for the blessings of God to be granted unto them, for His deliverance to be extended to them, and that their enemies might not have power to hold them in bondage; and the word of the Lord came to them and whispered peace, and told them that the day of their deliverance was nigh at hand, the day in which He would emancipate them from the thraldom of their enemies.

This is a good example for us to follow. It is possible for us to bring ourselves into such a condition that we can pray unto God in our hearts, no matter what labor we are performing. We are exhorted to pray constantly unto Him, and it is possible for us to concentrate our thoughts on the things of God while we are doing our labor, and our thanksgivings can ascend silently unto God, and they are not unheard by Him, and His blessing can descend upon us, and His joy can fill our hearts, and we can become the happiest and the most blessed people upon all the face of the earth.

I know it requires a struggle to concentrate our thoughts on the things of the kingdom of God, while we are engaged in business; but this is one of the things which we have to train ourselves to and to overcome.

George Q. Cannon 11:34

And all people of any age, race or country who seek unto God with an honest heart in fervent prayer, desiring truth and to be taught of God, will be enlightened by Him.

Charles W. Penrose 23:346
See also 8:65; 21:283; 24:129

Remember the Father and the Son

Now, can we live our religion unless we are in possession of the Holy Ghost all the time? We cannot. First, there is the Father, then the Son, and then the Holy Ghost; and then come faith, repentance, and baptism for the remission of sins, and laying on of hands for the gift of the Holy Ghost. . . . No man can please the Lord God, only as he is dictated by the Holy Ghost; and he will not stay with you unless you keep in view the Father and the Son. We partake of the sacrament every Sabbath to bear in remembrance the Son of God. . . .

Are these principles the celestial law? I know of no other. And how can you keep the celestial law without the Holy Ghost? You cannot. When you partake of the sacrament, you do it in remembrance of Jesus Christ, and of the Father, and of the Holy Ghost, and in remembrance that you have forsaken your sins and been baptised for the remission of them. Some may say, "How long will it be before the celestial law will be put into force?" Never, until you put it into force and execute it on yourselves.

Heber C. Kimball 6:122

Acknowledge Joseph Smith as a Prophet

They may say that they acknowledge Him [God] until doomsday, and he will never own them, nor bestow the Holy Spirit upon them, and they will never have visions of eternity opened to them, unless they acknowledge that Joseph Smith is sent of God. . . . The spirit that confesses that this is the kingdom of God and his Church has the Spirit that fills the heavenly worlds, and every other spirit is of Antichrist.

Brigham Young 8:177

Live in Harmony with the Holy Ghost

It is with the Holy Spirit as it is with us. When we seek to gratify ourselves in the associations around us, for whom do we seek in such a time? We seek individuals whose tastes and feelings are congenial to our own, whose "Mormonism" is like ours, whose regard for truth is like our own. Then what do we enjoy? A free, frank, unrestrained feeling and sentiment: we pour out the feelings of our souls; there is a principle of reciprocity existing between the parties.

So it is with the Holy Spirit of truth. Where it finds a mind so regulated that there is an affinity and congeniality between that mind and itself, there is the place where it will dwell; and when that mind becomes so trained in the truth as to be completely and perfectly subject to its influence, it will remain there constantly and unceasingly; it will not pay a casual visit, but take up its constant abode with that individual, and then its light is there, revelation is there, inspiration is there; it is there to increase in intensity, extent, and in power; it is there to continually pour out upon that soul the unceasing, unbroken tide of life.

Then the fountain of life becomes established in the soul; that fountain is flowing continually and unceasingly. Even as the blood passes through the heart to the extremities of our physical system at every pulsation, so also the Spirit of truth pervades our being.

Amasa M. Lyman 5:39-40

Do Will of God/Location Not Important

I do not and have not felt that I need a mission to a foreign land for the purpose of causing me to understand myself, or to fill me with the Holy Ghost, or to prepare me to be useful in this land; neither have I felt I needed to go to the United States or any other part of the world to put on the Gospel armor.

I feel it to be necessary that I should wear that armor here, and if I ever have had it on, I feel that I have had it on in this land; and I do not deem it necessary for many men to cross the ocean to get the Holy Ghost, or to enjoy the power of God. If they will do the will of God in this land, they will see their situation and be filled with His power from the crown of their heads to the soles of their feet; I believe that if the Saints were to have more religion in their own homes they would be better off.

Jedediah M. Grant 4:150

Labor to Obtain the Spirit

I would say to bishops, and to all men in authority, we should have an interest in carrying on this work. We should labor to get the Spirit of God. It is our right, our privilege, and our duty to call upon the Lord, that the vision of our mind may be opened, so that we may see and understand the day and age in which we are living. It is your privilege, and mine too, to know the mind and will of the Lord concerning our duties, and if we fail to seek after this, we neglect to magnify our calling.

Wilford Woodruff 21:283

Some people are very earnest after the things of God, and he who seeks finds, and the more he seeks in the right direction the more he finds. He that is dilatory in searching after the things of God, obtains but little; he that is diligent obtains much. All may receive it, but they must obtain it in the way that God has appointed, all receiving their measure according to their diligence and desire; but the spirit is the same.

Charles W. Penrose 24:88

Cultivate the Spirit of God That You Have

Now then, what shall we do? Continue to do good; continue to live our religion; continue to carry out the purposes of God; continue to humble ourselves before the Lord and cultivate his Holy Spirit that we may comprehend his laws and know his will concerning us.

You have received the Holy Ghost. Now I will tell you a piece of instruction that Joseph Smith once gave me, and it won't hurt you. Said he, "Elder Taylor, you have received the Holy Ghost: now follow the leadings of that spirit; and if you do, by-and-by it will become in you a principle of revelation that you will know all things as they come along and understand what is right and what is wrong in relation to them." That is just as applicable to you if you can receive it and live up to it and enjoy it.

John Taylor 20:227

We should strive to get faith in everything that pertains to this work, and feel that it rests upon our shoulders to perform, and that it behooves each one of us to live in that way that will promote our own interests therein, and give us light and knowledge, which will enable us to cultivate that Spirit in our bosoms which has been promised, as a well of water springing up into everlasting life, to all the faithful Saints. . . .

Let us nourish that kind Spirit in our bosoms, get light from the pure fountain, and not grieve it away by our unwise and sinful conduct. We frequently do things according to our feelings and opinions, until we in a great degree lose the light of the Spirit which should control, and which would, if we would let it, be a guide to our path and lead us in all that we do and say; and certainly we need it constantly to guide us and to enable us to render ourselves useful, and be the means of doing great good in the kingdom of God.

Daniel H. Wells 9:94, 95

And if you open a door that this Spirit will take up his abode with you, then that fountain which will be opened up will become very plenteous in its supplies; it will become so to you because you welcome the Holy Spirit there, and you study to cultivate within you such a feeling that the Spirit will love to tarry with you day by day; and its book of instructions will be opened to you, so that each succeeding day will give you an increase of knowledge, and you will find yourselves able to comprehend one degree of light and knowledge after another, until your whole soul will be swallowed up in your love for the truth; your affections will be bound up in the truth, for which you will be willing to sacrifice all. . . .

If the storm-clouds lour around you, you will be comforted by the sunshine of the Spirit of God. . . . Why will this be the case? Because you have prepared yourselves that the Spirit might be in you, having cultivated it all through your lives. Then you have a devotion to the truth, and the Spirit of truth will tarry with you, and by-and-by you will become fully devoted to the truth; your affections will become pure and holy; and then when you are purified and made holy, you will not depart from the truth; nor go into darkness and apostacy, because the sunlight of truth is within you.

Amasa M. Lyman 5:310

Now I want you to cultivate and cherish within you a love and regard for His Spirit. You have been exhorted again and again, so to live, that the Spirit of truth — the Holy Ghost, may dwell within you, and be your constant companion. You should cultivate that condition of feeling that is congenial with the Holy Spirit.

Amasa M. Lyman 3:174

Blow upon the spark of the Holy Ghost within you, and without which we need not anticipate building up the kingdom of God, that the wicked may be foiled in their efforts to corrupt and destroy. . . . Blow upon the spark that is within you; blow it as a flame, and see whether the fire of God's eternal love and the principles of the holy Gospel cannot be kindled with you.

Brigham Young 7:208
See also 5:70; 8:176; 23:352

Obey the Promptings of the Holy Ghost

This same spark of divinity, this monitor which speaks un-

mistakably to the understanding of the child, disapprovingly of his
wrong, will speak, in just as unmistakable language, approvingly of
good and righteous deeds. Therefore I know what I declare to be true,
because my conscience approves of my obeying the requirements of
the Gospel; this inward monitor testifies to my spirit that in rendering
this obedience I do right, and gives me the self-same assurance when I
am in the discharge of any other duties, whether officiating in the
capacity of an Elder or in the performance of those duties which, as an
individual, I owe to society.
    Joseph F. Smith 18:276

We are exhorted to make our own heaven, our own paradise, our
own Zion. How is this to be done? By hearkening diligently to the
voice of the Spirit of the Lord that entices to righteousness, applauds
truth, and exults continually in goodness.
    This Spirit is the companion of every faithful person! Listen to its
whisperings, and pursue with alacrity the path it points out. In this way
we may all grow in grace and in the knowledge of the truth, and by so
doing we shall honour the life we now possess, while by pursuing an
opposite course we disgrace it. This life is worth as much to us as any
life in the eternities of the Gods.
    Brigham Young 9:170

And I would say that it is the privilege of every Elder in Israel who
has received the gift of the Holy Ghost, to follow its teachings. What
was said by one of the old Apostles? "As many as are led by the Spirit
of God are the sons of God." Follow its teachings, therefore, and do
not give way to your own feelings, nor to covetousness, to pride, nor to
vain glory; for we none of us have anything to boast of.
    John Taylor 26:131

You ought to live so that the very moment the Spirit of the Lord is
grieved, stop that instantly, and turn the attention of every individual to
something else that will retain the good Spirit of the Lord and give you
an increase of it. This is the way to live.
    Brigham Young 14:205

I do not recollect that I have seen five minutes since I was baptized
that I have not been ready to preach a funeral sermon, lay hands on the
sick, or to pray in private or in public. I will tell you the secret of this.
In all your business transactions, words, and communications, if you
commit an overt act, repent of that immediately, and call upon God to
deliver you from evil and give you the light of His spirit.
    Never do a thing that your conscience, and the light within you, tell

you is wrong. Never do a wrong, but do all the good you possibly can. Never do a thing to mar the peaceable influence of the Holy Spirit in you; then whatever you are engaged in — whether in business, in the dance, or in the pulpit — you are ready to officiate at any time in any of the ordinances of the House of God.

> Brigham Young 12:103
> See also 5:172; 26:130-131

6

Living for the
Holy Ghost — Variances

Varies According to Their Efforts

As I look upon this congregation, and as I mingle with the Saints at large, I discover that there are different spirits. Every organization has a spirit peculiar to itself. I do not say that there is any fatality in this. Do not understand me to convey that idea. But I do say this, that every spirit connected with an earthly organization may be tempered by the Spirit of God according to its fidelity, intelligence, and faith, so that there is no excuse. . . .

Man is composed of matter and spirit; and the Spirit of God operates upon and tempers man's organization according to his faith and good works. Some are tempered very highly. Such not only carry a keen edge, but are susceptible of a high polish. Others are of low temper, because of a low, dull, and sluggish disposition and character, which they have indulged, and consequently formed. They are not a very smooth or sweet cutting tool. They have not sought to cultivate their temperament by seeking and courting the Spirit of God as they should.

Yet these may be guilty of no outbreaking sin. They keep within the pale of the law, pay their tithing, and keep along, and are considered good, peaceable, and honourable citizens. They despise to steal, are willing to labour, and pursue an even, straight-forward course. Still, we cannot look upon them as being tempered by the Holy Spirit to the extent of their privilege. Yet they work righteousness as far as they work at all. These persons are fond of going to meeting, and are often heard to say, "What a good sermon we have had!"

This is all right, if you did have a good sermon. They will ask you a thousand and one questions in order to draw out something to satisfy their eager desire for knowledge and understanding, not hardly recollecting their privilege to ask God and receive for themselves. But there is no crime in this. Still, one can hardly refrain from thinking, when he sees his neighbor begging and borrowing bread, how much more commendable it would be in him to apply himself to labour and produce, thereby, bread from the soil by his own exertion.

And inasmuch as our Heavenly Father is accessible to all, it is far better to store our minds with the treasures of wisdom and knowledge, by our own spiritual labours and toil, direct from the great Fountain of celestial light and love, than to trust wholly to the testimony and teachings of others. Obtain the testimony of Jesus, which is the spirit of prophecy. Startle not at the idea of prophecy and prophets; for I would to God that all the Lord's people were prophets.

> Orson Hyde 5:70-71

Now, although there are a variety of operations of this spirit, yet the spirit is the same and the light that it brings is the same. People do not all receive that light to the same degree, but the light is the same, just as the light of the sun is the same to all. Some people can see a great deal further than others with their natural eyes. Their eyesight is better, but the light by which both see is the same.

So it is with regard to the gift of the Holy Ghost. All people do not receive it in the same degree, because they are not all gifted with the same capacity, and all have not the same desires; but the difference is not in the spirit, it is in the individual. Some people are very earnest after the things of God, and he who seeks finds, and the more he seeks in the right direction the more he finds. He that is dilatory in searching after the things of God, obtains but little; he that is diligent obtains much.

All may receive it, but they must obtain it in the way that God has appointed, all receiving their measure according to their diligence and desire; but the spirit is the same. And this spirit has operated upon our hearts in such a way as to make us — a people of diverse feelings and opinions — of one heart and one mind in regard to this matter.

> Charles W. Penrose 24:88
> See also 8:306

Many LDS Do Not Live for the Spirit

Of the Latter-day Saints there will be many who will not so live their religion as to fully enjoy the Holy Ghost. The Latter-day Saints are like children who have to be taught continually, and still, like children, they handle, figuratively speaking, razors, glasses, cups, saucers, etc. contrary to the teachings that are given them.

Brigham Young 8:177

He [President Jedediah M. Grant] said that after he came back [from a visit to the Spirit World] he could look upon his family and see the spirit that was in them, and the darkness that was in them; and that he conversed with them about the Gospel, and what they should do, and they replied, "Well, brother Grant, perhaps it is so, and perhaps it is not," and said that was the state of this people, to a great extent, for many are full of darkness and will not believe me.

Heber C. Kimball 4:136

7

One's Spirit
Should Control Body

Two Forces in the World

Here we are subjected to the power of the adversary. He can tempt us; try us. Satan has power in the earth, and in the exercise of his agency he tempts the children of men. He has rebelled against God in the exercise of his agency; for he was a great and a mighty angel in the presence of our Father and our God. But in the exercise of his agency he rebelled against the Father and drew away with him one-third of the hosts of heaven, who likewise exercised their agency and followed him in preference to following the Lord God, their Father; and in the continued exercise of his agency he tempts us. He has power over us to that extent in this fallen condition.

At the same time, we have the sweet influence of the Spirit of God pleading with us to do that which is right, pleading with every human being that does not drive it from him; for every human being has a portion of the Spirit of God unto him. We sometimes call it conscience; we call it by one name and we call it by another; but it is the Spirit of God that every man and woman possesses that is born on the earth. God has given unto all his children this Spirit.

Of course it is not the gift of the Holy Ghost in its fullness; for that is only received by obedience to the commandments of God — to the Gospel of our Lord and Savior Jesus Christ. But it is a Spirit that pleads with men to do right. . . . It pleads with man to resist the blandishments of Satan. No man ever did a wrong but that Spirit warned him of it to a greater or less extent. No man ever put his hand forth to do a wrong to his neighbor without that Spirit telling him it was wrong. He never put forth his hand or influence to wrong the gentler sex — to commit sin in that direction — without that warning voice which is in every human being telling him of the sin.

On the other hand, there is the influence of evil, the influence of the Adversary enticing men to do wrong, leading into paths of sin, leading them away from righteousness and from God; infusing doubt, infusing unbelief, infusing hardness of heart, infusing rebellion against everything that is holy and pure.

We are all conscious of the existence of these two influences within us. There is no child that has reached the age of accountability and in the possession of his or her faculties but what has had these two influences pleading with him or her — one entreating to do right, the other enticing to do wrong, to commit sin and to violate the commandments of God. If we cultivate the good influence it will lead us into the truth (if we are not already in possession of the truth) when we hear it.

> George Q. Cannon 26:191-192

When the Spirit of the Lord rests upon a community, they naturally are inclined to feel after the Lord their God, and they are inclined unto righteousness, and they like the influence of that Spirit which leads into all truth; it is sweet and very delicious to them. But when darkness beclouds the people in consequence of their transgressions, they have but little relish for the things of God; they relish every thing else but the things which pertain to the kingdom of God on the earth, and the kingdom of God hereafter.

They cannot enjoy the Gospel as do those who are not in the dark, for those who are in the light can appreciate the light they are in enjoyment of. But while people are in the dark, they do not see the light; their deeds are not made manifest, for it is the light that maketh manifest. If a room be dark, the objects in that room are not discernible, but when light breaks into the room, the objects therein can be plainly seen.

We may say the same of the people of God; when they are in the dark, no difference how much light they may have had, if they pass from the light into the dark, they may remember that they once saw the light, they do not enjoy the light because they have passed from light into darkness, and they do not discern the objects in themselves. They gradually are sliding from the law of God, or from the Church of God, and do not discover where they are going or what from, from the fact that they are in the dark, they cannot see. . . .

But if light breaks forth from any source and reflects upon the people, they then see the motes, the beams, and the dross in themselves. While the light maketh manifest, the Spirit of God reveals the secrets of the heart, and makes manifest those dark spots that exist among the Saints of God.

> Jedediah M. Grant 4:123
> See also 2:255-256; 5:328

Your Spirit

A. Communications to Your Spirit

Your parents can approach you through your natural senses; they address themselves to the tabernacle. But when we come to the constitution of the spirit that dwells within the tabernacle, and then come to understand that that spirit emanated from God the Father, to whom will God the Father speak? Will He speak to the tabernacle that is the result of the agency of man and woman in producing it? No, only seldom and then to chosen ones, God the Father speaks to his own; and the angels that minister and speak, address themselves to the mind, as we call it, to this spirit that cannot be seen, that cannot be handled, that cannot be heard by the ears of the natural man.

Here is the grand difficulty with the human family today. God cannot speak to them for they want to compel Him to come down to the grossness of the earthly tabernacle and reason everything out to the sense of that tabernacle. He will not do it. He did not six thousand years ago; and He will not do it now, nor in all time to come.

The very medium through which inspiration comes, the very medium through which knowledge comes that benefits the human family, no matter whether it be scientific, philosophical or otherwise, there is not a truth extant upon the earth today that has been utilized, or many truths combined together that have been utilized, but have been the result of divine inspiration directly to the spirit of man, to the mind of man which is sometimes incorrectly called the soul of Man.

God will talk with His own creation, and if that spirit in man will place itself in a position to listen to the voice of God, what will he say to that spirit, "Control that tabernacle, I gave it to you for a greater exaltation. . . ."

> Joseph E. Taylor 23:247

B. Satan's Limitations Unless Man Yields to the Flesh

When the spirit enters the body, it is pure and holy from the heavens; and could it reign predominantly in the tabernacle, ruling, dictating, and directing its actions without an opposing force, man never would commit a sin; but the tabernacle has to suffer the effects of the fall, of that sin which Satan has introduced into the world and hence the spirit does not bear rule all the time.

Brigham Young 9:287

You are aware that many think that the devil has rule and power over both body and spirit. Now, I want to tell you that he does not hold any power over man, only so far as the body overcomes the spirit that is in a man, through yielding to the spirit of evil. The spirit that the Lord puts into a tabernacle of flesh, is under the dictation of the Lord Almighty; but the spirit and body are united in order that the spirit may have a tabernacle, and be exalted; and the spirit is influenced by the body, and the body by the spirit.

In the first place the spirit is pure, and under the special control and influence of the Lord, but the body is of the earth, and is subject to the power of the devil, and is under the mighty influence of that fallen nature that is of the earth. If the spirit yields to the body, the devil then has power to overcome both the body and spirit of that man, and he loses both.

Brigham Young 2:255-256

C.   Our Spirit's Responsibility for the Body

The spirit is held responsible for the acts done in the body. No spirit can plead, before the bar of Jehovah, the weakness of the flesh as a justification of sin; the latter may be urged in palliation, but not in justification.

Our Father is full of mercy, but he cannot look upon sin in any individual with the least degree of allowance; but every spirit must be held responsible, and will have to answer at the bar of God, and will there receive a just and righteous judgment for the deeds done in the body.

Erastus Snow 13:8

Our spirits will not go down into the grave. They live in the presence of God; they will be held responsible for that tabernacle, for its acts, for its development; they will be held responsible before God, before the heavens, for the faith they have exercised, or for the wrongs that they have allowed themselves to be guilty of in the flesh.

Joseph E. Taylor 23:249

D.   The Need to Control Our Bodies

It is the business of the spirit to preside over, to be master of and to control this fleshy tabernacle to all intents and purposes and to hold it subject to all the laws of God.

Joseph E. Taylor 23:249

This tabernacle is formed expressly to hold its spirit and shield it. Should we love this tabernacle? Yes, enough to nourish it, cherish it, and treat it kindly, and foster and nourish and cherish it by the power of the spirit, and make this body divine. The spirit must overcome the body in the flesh, and the flesh become subject to the spirit in all things; then we will love the world as it ought to be loved — not with a divine love, but with a human love, a moral love, loving all things according to their worth and capacity.

We love our wives and children — we love that which is calculated to make us happy and comfortable; but the divine spirit is to overcome the body and continue so to do, looking forth until the body also becomes divine; and then, when all has become divine, we may love all with a divine affection, but not till then.

Brigham Young 9:139

When we receive the Gospel, a warfare commences immediately; Paul says, "For I delight in the law of God, after the inward man, but I see another law in my members warring against the law of my mind, and bringing me into captivity to the law of sin which is in my members."

We have to fight continually, as it were, sword in hand to make the spirit master of the tabernacle, or the flesh subject to the law of the spirit. If this warfare is not diligently prosecuted, then the law of sin prevails, and in consequence of this some apostatize from the truth when crossing the plains, learn to swear instead of to pray, become highminded and high tempered instead of learning to be patient and humble, and when they arrive in these vallies they feel so self-sufficient that they consider themselves the only ones that are really right; they are filled with darkness, the authority of the Spirit is not listened to, and the law of sin and death is the ruling power in their tabernacles. . . .

The rule of the flesh brings darkness and death, while, on the other hand, the rule of the Spirit brings light and life. When through the Gospel, the Spirit in man has so subdued the flesh that he can live without wilful transgression, the Spirit of God unites with his spirit, they become congenial companions, and the mind and will of the Creator is thus transmitted to the creature.

Brigham Young 9:287-288

E.   The Spirit and the Body After the Resurrection

God will talk with His own creation, and if that spirit in man will place itself in a position to listen to the voice of God, what will he say to that spirit, "Control that tabernacle, I gave it to you for a greater exaltation; I gave it to you that after it shall have passed away, it may be resurrected from the grave, and if you subdue its passions, its unholy desires, if you sanctify that tabernacle before Me, then I am bound to bring that tabernacle from the grave and to bring it to the enjoyment of the fullness of My glory, which was the destiny of the spirit when it was first created.''

        Joseph E. Taylor 23:247

But, says one, there are weaknesses that pertain to the flesh, are they all sins? No. What about those weaknesses? The man who has been pure in his spirit, pure in his heart, pure in his intentions and desires before God, when he lays that body down in the grave there will be found in the very elements with which his body will mingle, a power to cleanse and purify all weaknesses as pertaining to the flesh which cannot be regarded as sins before God.

Yes, give mother earth time and she will so effectually purify the tabernacle that she will get it ready for the resurrection from the grave to be reunited with the Spirit. Then after a while we shall become acquainted with the higher laws, with principles altogether different to those taught to us in the flesh and which also pertain to eternal lives.

And then again, when we come to be resurrected from the grave we shall find other conditions in advance of those; we shall find God's Priesthood there, his law there, his power there, his influence there, as there will be teachings and instructions to be given even then; and thus shall we keep going on from condition to condition of perfection and glory until we become possessed of the glory that belongs to God.

Is it worth living for? Is it worth enduring a few threats for? Is it worth being quiet when you are menaced, and as passive as the Lord wants you to be? Yes. Is it worth making any sacrifice for? Is it worth leaving home, father, mother, sister, brother? It is. And why?

The day will come, perchance, even in the spirit world, when that father and mother, sister and brother, who despised you, will be seeking after salvation and will want to have conferred upon them the powers of eternal life. And you will have placed yourself in the position to act for them though your body may be in the grave, for your spirit still lives and you can preach and even become a minister of salvation to those of your own house. Amen.

        Joseph E. Taylor 23:249

After the body and spirit are separated by death, what, pertaining to this earth, shall we receive first? The body; that is the first object of a divine affection beyond the grave. We first come in possession of the body. The Spirit has overcome the body, and the body is made subject in every respect to that divine principle God has planted in the person.

The spirit within is pure and holy, and goes back pure and holy to God, dwells in the spirit-world pure and holy, and, by-and-by, will have the privilege of coming and taking the body again. Some person holding the keys of the resurrection, having previously passed through that ordeal, will be delegated to resurrect our bodies, and our spirits will be there and prepared to enter into their bodies. Then, when we are prepared to receive our bodies, they are the first earthly objects that bear divinity personified in the capacity of the man.

Brigham Young 9:139

How to Gain Strength over Your Flesh

A. Resist Evil

When a person receives the Holy Ghost by legal authority, he is like a child in its mother's lap; all is harmony, praise to God, and good will to the children of men on the earth. He is full of peace, comfort, and salvation, and feels like crying hallelujah all the time. He is perfectly humble and passive, and the Lord can do with him as He pleases.

Will this state of feeling always remain? Will passion ever rise again? Yes; for you then commence a warfare, though the Comforter fills your heart, making you rejoice in God your Savior, with the atmosphere of your existence clear and unclouded; this is not to continue, but soon the day of trial and temptation darkens the fair prospect, to teach you to lean on the Lord, and to overcome the world.

Under the influence of the Holy Ghost I have felt as happy as I possibly could feel, my heart has been full of joy; I cling to that, and hold fast to the promise of the Lord in the hour of temptation, and call upon Him to give me strength to overcome.

Brigham Young 1:240-241

If he continues day after day to yield himself a servant to the uncontrolled whims of his own nature and the evil influences that may be exercised upon him from without, in a few years he will be so steeped in sin as to be entirely given over to the error of his ways. The sooner an individual resists temptation to do, say, or think wrong, while he has light to correct his judgment, the quicker he will gain strength and power to overcome every temptation to evil.

Brigham Young 6:94

See also 6:207; 12:103; (this excellent quotation is in "Obey the Promptings of the Holy Ghost," chapter 5)

B. How to Resist Evil

Recollect, brethren and sisters, every one of you, that when evil is suggested to you, when it arises in your hearts, it is through the temporal organization. When you are tempted, buffetted, and step out of the way inadvertently; when you are overtaken in a fault, or commit an overt act unthinkingly; when you are full of evil passion, and wish to yield to it, then stop and let the spirit, which God has put into your tabernacles, take the lead.

If you do that, I will promise that you will overcome all evil, and obtain eternal lives. But many, very many, let the spirit yield to the body, and are overcome and destroyed.

The influence of the enemy has power over all such. Those who overcome every passion, and every evil, will be sanctified, and be prepared to enjoy eternity with the blessed. If you have never thought of this before, try to realize it now. Let it rest upon your minds, and see if you can discover in yourselves the operations of the spirit and the body, which constitute the man. Continually and righteously watch the spirit that the Lord has put in you, and I will promise you to be led into righteousness, holiness, peace, and good order.

But let the body rise up with its passions, with the fallen nature pertaining to it, and let the spirit yield to it, your destruction is sure. On the other hand, let the spirit take the lead, and bring the body and its passions into subjection, and you are safe.

    Brigham Young 2:256

If you will always keep your spirits in right subjection, you will be watching all the time, and never suffer yourselves to commit an act that you will be sorry for, and you can see that in all your life you are clear. Do not do anything that you will be sorry for.

    Brigham Young 5:328

Why not in the same way, institute a proper and salutary correction over the rebellious spirit that at times arises in the human breast? Why not govern and control the appetite, that it may be subject to the law of Christ? But how is it? Why, "I must have some tobacco, if I am damned for it." Or, "I must have a cup of tea, if I am damned for it." Or, "I must have this or that, if I should have to go to hell for it."

It is like saying to our Heavenly Father, "I will not mind you, I will not obey your commandments, but I will have my own way and follow the bent of my own inclinations; my appetite shall be nursed and pampered, though it be at the expense of your displeasure." Instead of pursuing this course, listen to that Spirit God has given to all, which teaches the right and how to avoid the wrong, and say to appetite, to disposition, to temper, to the whole man, you must do as I command you; I am an officer, a general in the army of Christ and I will be obeyed.

Every man and woman is called to the same office; let us magnify it, and exert a mighty influence over this organization, and rise up in the strength of the great I Am, and by the power of his eternal Priesthood, command every power, every pulse of our natures to be subject to the law of God and truth. . . .

If men are ruled by the power, principles and righteousness of the Holy Priesthood, they will find themselves in possession of all the wisdom they need to meet every emergency of this changing existence, and all they require to conquer the world, the flesh, and the Devil.

> Brigham Young 9:257

And if any are disposed to let that unruly member, the tongue, do that which will wound the heart, darken the spirit, and bring us into subjection to an evil practice, resist such a disposition — throw it from you.

If you will do that, you will find that the wicked will forsake their wickedness, and those who are inclined to think evil will cease doing so, and those who are inclined to utter evil words about their neighbors will cease that habit, and it will not be long before the people have perfect control over themselves.

If you first gain power to check your words, you will then begin to have power to check your judgment, and at length actually gain power to check your thoughts and reflections.

> Brigham Young 6:98

Would the principles of the Gospel, if obeyed, teach us to control ourselves? They would. They will teach men and women to govern and control their own passions.

You very frequently hear it said, "Such a man or woman has too much temper." This is a mistaken idea. No person on earth has too much of this article. But do we not frequently see the evil conduct of people through allowing their passions and tempers to have full control of them? Certainly we do. What is the difficulty?

We want the spirit, knowledge, power and principle within us to govern and control our tempers; there is no danger of having too much if we will only control them by the Spirit of the Almighty. Every intelligent being on the earth is tempered for glory, beauty, excellency and knowledge here, and for immortality and eternal lives in the worlds to come. But every being who attains to this must be sanctified before God and be completely under the control of His Spirit.

If I am thus controlled by the Spirit of the Most High I am King, I am supreme so far as the control of self is concerned; and it also enables me to control my wife and children. And when they thus see that I am under the government and control of the Good Spirit, they will be perfectly submissive to my dictates. They feel and say, "Yes, father, or husband, certainly, you never require anything that is wrong; I have learned that long ago. Your judgment and discretion and the power of thought and reflection in you are sufficient; you know what is right."

And if I could extend this power I could reign supreme, not only over my family and friends, but also over my neighbors and the people all around me. Could the spirit of error, hatred and wickedness perform this? No, it can be accomplished only by means of the meek and humble spirit of the Lord Jesus. If an individual is filled with that, it makes him a perfect monarch over himself, and it will give him influence over all who will hearken to his counsel.

Brigham Young 13:272

We get angry, we get out of humor, "out of sorts," as the printers term it; hence we do not have that equanimity of thought which it is desirable that we should possess. Our passions rule us, and we do not rule them; the passions, the feelings that may be within us, overcome us, and we say we did not think anything about it.

We do not think that we are to control ourselves, that this is our business upon the earth, that we came here to learn our Father and the principles which influence him — to learn how he has put on power, and how he has surrounded himself with glory and strength, come off victorious, and never become subject to evil.

Well, are we learning it when our passions are running away with us like a wild, untrained team with the carriages that they are attached to?

Amasa M. Lyman 5:309

As brother Amasa said, the Lord has a school upon the earth, and we are his scholars; and the Devil also has a school attended by a great number of scholars. While we have been learning how to sustain the kingdom of God upon the earth, the Devil and his pupils have been learning how to sustain the kingdom of darkness.

From the very nature of the two kingdoms upon one planet, the crisis must come when there will be a literal open warfare, just as much as there now is a warfare within us against evil; and if we, as individuals and as a community, have gained the victory over our passions to such a degree that our Father knows that we are capable of actually sustaining the kingdom of God upon the earth, just so true we shall be a kingdom by ourselves. If we are not yet capable of maintaining and rightly managing that kingdom, it will not at present be given to us in the fulness thereof; but the time will come when it will be given and established in its perfect organization on the earth.

A great many — yes, the most of this people have kept up a spiritual warfare until they have become almost masters of their passions; yet we still see some of them who do sin. . . . Keep your spirits in subject to the principles of truth and life, and do not let evil spirits control you.

> Brigham Young 5:328
> See also 1:240-241; 7:314; 11:134; 23:247

You want to live so that your minds will be filled with his Spirit. . . . Are you acquainted with your homes? You answer, "Yes." Well, then, do right at home, do not do wrong, do not quarrel at home, do not stir up disunion, do not, in a word, do anything to bring about a pandemonium instead of a paradise; but do that which brings peace — that which produces the spirit of peace and of heaven.

But where division of sentiment, diversity of feeling, and discord exist, the principles of heaven are not there; the principles of peace are not there.

> Amasa M. Lyman 5:310

The Book of Mormon, of Doctrine and Covenants, the Old and New Testaments all corroborate the fact that when you receive the Spirit that gives you light, intelligence, peace, joy, and comfort, that it is from God.

But when you, sisters, particularly in your family affairs, are tried and tempted, when parents and children have a spirit come upon them that irritates them, that causes them to have bad feelings, disagreeable, unhappy, and miserable sensations, causing them to say, "We wish it was some way else; we wish our circumstances were different; we are not happy; something or the other is always wrong; we wish to do just right, but we are very unhappy;" I desire to tell you that your own conduct is the cause of all this.

"But," says one, "I have done nothing wrong, nothing evil." No matter whether you have or not, you have given way to a spirit of temptation. There is not that man or woman in this congregation, or on the face of the earth, that has the privilege of the Holy Gospel, and lives strictly to it, whom all hell can make unhappy. You cannot make the man, woman, or child unhappy, who possesses the Spirit of the living God; unhappiness is caused by some other spirit.

The spirit of contention divides families as we see some divided. We can hardly associate with some persons, for we have to walk in their midst like walking upon eggs. What is the matter? You do not know the spirit they are led by.

Treat them kindly, and, perhaps, by and by they will come to understanding. What would they do were they of one heart and mind? They would be like little children, would respect their superiors and honor their God and their religion. This they would do, if they understood things as they are. Be careful of them, and treat them kindly.

Brigham Young 3:343

I must break from the thread of my discourse here, and say — Husbands, is that the way you do? Wives, do you adopt that plan when passion arises in your hearts against each other? Do you call upon the name of Jesus Christ, and say, "Father, I ask thee for the gift of thy Spirit to conquer this rising passion;" or do you give way to it, and scold at your wife, or at your children, in bitter and vindictive language?

Brigham Young 1:241

I know that it may be said, and with great propriety, "Why, my brother, we can not be sanctified in one day, we cannot overcome every evil and every passion in one day." That is true, but this holy desire can dwell in the heart of every individual from the time that he or she is convinced that God reigns, that he is establishing his kingdom on the earth, that Jesus is our Savior, that the holy Gospel has presented to us the way of life and salvation, and we believe it and can receive it with our whole hearts.

I say we can have that holy and pure desire from that moment to the end of our lives, and in possessing this we have faith and favor before the Lord, and his grace is with us by the power of his Holy Spirit, and by this we can overcome temptations as we meet them. This is my experience, that is pretty good proof, is it not?

Brigham Young 16:27

As every person in his experience knows that the spirit wars against the flesh, and the flesh against the spirit. So far as our spirits by the power of God, by the Holy Ghost — by the Spirit of the Lord Jesus, are assisted to overcome every seed of iniquity and sin within us, we may expect to gain the victory over our evil passions; and in that proportion this people will gain victory in a national capacity.

Brigham Young 5:328

But be careful that you do not lose it! Live so that you will know the moment the Spirit of the Almighty is grieved within you. . . . You ought to live so that the very moment the Spirit of the Lord is grieved, stop that instantly, and turn the attention of every individual to something else that will retain the good Spirit of the Lord and give you an increase of it. This is the way to live.

Brigham Young 14:205
See also 2:256; 14:135; 26:191

Summary

When through the Gospel, the Spirit in man has so subdued the flesh that he can live without wilful transgression, the Spirit of God unites with his spirit, they become congenial companions, and the mind and will of the Creator is thus transmitted to the creature.

Brigham Young 9:288

They receive that which was promised by the Savior when he was about to leave the earth, namely, the Comforter. . . . And the fact that we receive this Comforter, the Holy Ghost, is proof that the spirit in warring with the flesh has overcome, and by continuing in this state of victory over our sinful bodies we become the sons and daughters of God, Christ having made us free, and whoever the Son makes free is free indeed.

Brigham Young 18:259

When the spirit overcomes the evil consequences of the fall, which are in the mortal tabernacle, it will reign predominant in the flesh, and is then prepared to be exalted, and will, in the resurrection, be reunited with those particles that formed the mortal body, which will be called together as with the sound of a trumpet and become immortal. Why? Because the particles composing these bodies have been made subject and obedient, by the law of the everlasting Priesthood, and the will and commandment of the Supreme Ruler of the universe, who holds the keys of life and death.

Brigham Young 7:287

8

We Need
the Holy Ghost

Again, the theocracy I speak of is the power of the Holy Ghost within you — that living and eternal principle that we do not possess in the fulness that we are seeking.

Brigham Young 6:347

Need Every Day of Our Lives

And if we will so live before the Lord, the Spirit will reveal to us every day what our duties are; I do not care what it is we are engaged in, we should first find out the will of the Lord and then do it, and then our work will be well done and acceptable before the Lord, but if we take a course against light and against the Spirit of God, we will find it an unprofitable road to travel.

Wilford Woodruff 4:230

This people that were not a people have become a people, even the people of God. They must have the bread of life continually as well as those who administer unto them in the word of life. We not only need it who rise up to preach, but every man and woman needs it; they need it in their families; they need fresh supplies from heaven by the ministrations of the Holy Ghost daily, hourly, and every moment, to qualify them for their duties.

Franklin D. Richards 5:45

The Elders of Israel, though the great majority of them are moral men, and as clear of spot and blemish as men well can be, live beneath their privilege; they live continually without enjoying the power of God. I want to see men and women breathe the Holy Ghost in every breath of their lives, living constantly in the light of God's countenance.

Brigham Young 9:288-289

Our business is then to find out what the Lord's will is, to guide us in our everyday life, not only to make us feel good, to exalt our spiritual nature, our emotions, our sentiments, our thoughts, not only that, but to guide us in our daily lives, so that all our acts may be squared according to the rule of right, that we may do that which is pleasing to our Heavenly Father, that we may learn to live so as not merely to do our own will, but to do the will of Him that has sent us here on the earth, and who has enlightened our minds in regard to the truth. We need not walk in the dark. It is our privilege to walk in the light.

Charles W. Penrose 25:46-47

It is not enough, then, that we are baptized and have hands laid upon us for the gift of the Holy Ghost. It is not enough even that we go further than this, and receive our washing and our anointings, but that we daily and hourly and all the time live up to our religion, cultivate the Spirit of God, and have it continually within us "as a well of water springing up unto everlasting life," unfolding, developing, making manifest the purposes and designs of God unto us, that we may be enabled to walk worthy of the high avocation whereunto we are called, as sons and daughters of God to whom he has committed the principles of eternal truth and the oracles of God in these last days.

John Taylor 6:106-107
See also 5:309, 368; 8:176; 10:296; 18:99, 100; 20:234

Need in Every Phase of Our Lives

The world could not hire me to be a "Mormon," unless I enjoyed the spirit of my religion. I need that spirit in my business, as well as in my worship; and I surely would need it, if I had to go to the kanyons and drive cattle: I would need a double portion of it. Whatever we do should be in accordance with the mind of the Holy Spirit.

Brigham Young 7:271

There is not a position that we can occupy in life, either as fathers, mothers, children, masters, servants, or as Elders of Israel holding the holy Priesthood in all its ramifications, but what we need continually wisdom flowing from the Lord and intelligence communicated by him, that we may know how to perform correctly the various duties and avocations of life, and to fulfill the various responsibilities that rest upon us.

And hence the necessity all the day long, and every day and every week, month, and year, and under all circumstances, of men leaning upon the Lord and being guided by that Spirit that flows from him, that we may not fall into error — that we may neither do anything wrong, say anything wrong, nor think anything wrong, and all the time retain that Spirit, which can only be kept by observing purity, holiness, and virtue, and living continually in obedience to the laws and commandments of God.

John Taylor 6:106

If men cannot study and practice law and keep the Spirit of the Lord, they ought to quit it. As I have frequently told the people at our places of recreation, if they cannot go there with the Spirit of the Lord, they had better stay at home. We do not want lawyers, nor merchants, nor business men to be engaged in those pursuits unless they have the Spirit of God with them.

We do not wish them to continue in their business unless they can see and understand that all things pertaining to this earth are subject by right to the priesthood of God, and should be guided and directed by it in every matter. All that they are, have, or do, ought to be subject to the priesthood of the Son of God; and unless they can feel thus, they had better go into the fields and canyons to work — suffer themselves to be poor and keep the Holy Spirit with them.

Brigham Young 11:283

There is but one way to be united, according to the will of God, and that is by being dictated in our affairs by the Spirit of the Lord. . . . We have need of revelation at every step after we are baptized, for when we take a step it ought to be a right step.

Charles C. Rich 19:252

There is one point we should be guarded against, and the brethren have endeavored to impress it upon our minds, that is, in our seeking to develop the resources of the earth and build up cities and temples and the various works that are incumbent on us, that we should not forget to keep our minds right before the Lord, that we should have his Holy Spirit abiding within us.

When the cares of every day life increase upon us, in the business of forming settlements, pioneering and performing our labors from day to day, we are too apt to forget that we should constantly seek to God with the same fervor and diligence for His aid as we do for spiritual blessings.

I find that I have to be careful while engaged in business, for I know that the tendency of my mind is to devote all my thoughts and all my time and attention to the business that is in hand — that happens to occupy my attention at the time. This is the tendency of people generally, and we have to guard against it, and for which we have to be reproved, that we may not yield to it to so great an extent as to drive the spirit of God from us. There is no necessity for this.

If we grieve the Spirit of God when we are performing our temporal duties, it is because we allow the one idea to absorb our attention too much. While we are engaged in these duties, we should have the Spirit of God resting upon us, as if we are engaged in preaching the Gospel.

George Q. Cannon 11:33-34

For as it is written, an actual knowledge to any person, that the course of life which he pursues is according to the will of God, is essentially necessary to enable him to have that confidence in God without which no person can obtain eternal life. For unless a person does know that he is walking according to the will of God, it would be an insult to the dignity of the Creator were he to say that he would be a partaker of his glory when he should be done with the things of this life.

But when he has this knowledge, and most assuredly knows that he is doing the will of God, his confidence can be equally strong that he will be a partaker of the glory of God.

Joseph F. Smith 19:23

I will take the liberty of saying that it is your privilege, brethren, to get the mind and will of the Lord in relation to your duties while abroad among the people; and it is also the privilege of the whole people who are called Israel to obtain the revelations of the Holy Spirit to guide them in every duty in life.

Whatever position a man may stand in, it is his privilege, as a Saint of God, to enjoy this blessing; and a man who understands himself will not move without the operations of that Spirit to lead him.

Wilford Woodruff 5:85
See also 25:60

9

Why We Need the
Holy Ghost Continually

Guide Us in Our Lives

The Scriptures inform us "that no man knows the things of God, but by the Spirit of God;" and then no man can speak the things of God unless aided by the Spirit of the Lord; and no people can comprehend the things spoken unless inspired and guided by the same spirit.

We need this Spirit continually and so do all mankind, to guide us, to enable us to comprehend the laws of life, to regulate and concentrate our thoughts, to elevate and ennoble our feelings, to give force and vitality to our actions, and to place us in a position before God, before men, and before the holy angels, that will be right, acceptable and proper to all true intelligence, to the angelic host, and to our heavenly Father.

It matters very little what we are engaged in, it is impossible for us to do right without the guidance of the Almighty; but aided and directed by the Spirit of the Lord, we can act in consonance with the dignity of our high position as immortal beings possessing the holy Priesthood, and participating in the new and everlasting covenant; by the aid of that unerring Spirit we can fulfill the measure of our creation and prepare ourselves for an inheritance in the celestial kingdom of our God.

John Taylor 13:221

But it is our privilege also to receive the word of the Lord direct to ourselves each in our individual sphere and capacity, for we hold a relationship to God as individuals, as well as a community. It is our privilege if we live aright, each one for himself to receive direct from the fountain of life, intelligence, wisdom and knowledge for our individual guidance, inspiration to direct us in all things that we are called upon to perform.

The father of a family has a right to receive the inspiration of the Holy Ghost to direct him in all things pertaining to his household, to give words of wisdom and counsel to his wives and his children and all within the sphere of his authority and influence. It is the privilege of every mother to have the spirit of the Lord to direct her in the course she shall take with her children.

And it is the privilege of every boy and girl, who has been baptized into the Church, to receive the Holy Ghost for their guidance, so that the whole Church may be quickened, bodily and spiritually, with that life that comes from above; so that God may be able to impress us as individuals with desires and intelligence for the accomplishment of his purposes.

And we should so live as to be in harmony with the authorities of the Church; in harmony with those who preside over us, that we may be able to see as they see, and act as they desire us to act when they give us the word of the Lord. But we cannot do that unless we possess this spirit. And not only should we be in harmony with those men, but with the powers behind the vail; and we should be so tuned that our whole natures will be in perfect accord with the influences that come from on high, and be sensitive to the impressions God intends to make upon us.

Charles W. Penrose 21:46-47

Help Us Avoid Making Mistakes

There are many things pertaining to our everyday duties, which if we clearly understood by the light of the Spirit, we would escape many things which cause unhappiness. It is the want of clearly understanding the will of the Lord under all circumstances that causes us to fall into many of the evils that we pass through in life.

I can look back on my past life and can speak from experience in these matters. I can remember many times when, if I had been guided by the Spirit of the Lord in regard to temporal matters, it would have been well with me; but not altogether understanding what the mind of the Spirit was, the course I have taken at times has been very disadvantageous to me. . . . I can see, also, many times when the Spirit of the Lord whispered to me, and I scarcely knew whether it was my own thoughts and imaginations or whether it was the revelations of the

Spirit; yet it seemed to be the Spirit of the Lord, and I followed the teachings, and was prospered in so doing.

If we, as a people, would live up to our privileges, how many difficulties might be avoided! How many Latter-day Saints would constantly live in the light of revelation! . . . The idea is that in these tabernacles of ours we have an intelligent spirit which God has placed there, and he has ordained that the Spirit of the Lord shall light up these human spirits of ours, that we may follow in the paths of light, truth, and righteousness and obtain eternal life.

> Orson Pratt 15:230

We need assistance. We are liable to do that which will lead us into trouble and darkness, and those things which will not tend to our good, but with the assistance of that comforter which the Lord has promised his Saints, if we are careful to listen to its whisperings, and understand the nature of its language, we may avoid much trouble and serious difficulty.

> Lorenzo Snow 19:341

Salvation should be the uppermost thing with us, and you will find if ever we seek to do something else besides carrying out the dictates of the Holy Spirit, we will get into the fog and into darkness and trouble, and we shall be ignorant of the way we are pursuing. Every day that we live we need the power of the Lord — the power of His Holy Spirit and the strength of the Priesthood to be with us that we may know what to do.

> Wilford Woodruff 4:229-230

Aid in Our Church Callings

It is not possible for us to perform the labors that are required of us as Latter-day Saints — to preach the Gospel among the nations, to gather together the people, to build temples, and to perform in those temples the labors that are necessary for the salvation of the living and the dead — except we are aided by the Holy Ghost, the Comforter.

It is not possible for men who stand at the head of this Church to direct, or to give counsel in regard to the building up of the Kingdom of God, in regard to the location of new settlements, in regard to organizing branches, wards, and stakes, and the opening of missions, except they enjoy the Holy Ghost. It is not possible for us as Apostles, as Presidents of Stakes, as Bishops of wards, as Presidents of quorums, as Presidents of associations, to preside with dignity and in a manner pleasing to God, unless we enjoy the Holy Ghost. . . .

It was conferred upon every one of us when we were baptized, when we first embraced the Gospel, and the Lord has given us ample instructions as to how we should live, as to the labors we should perform, and as to the lives we should lead in order that we may enjoy the Holy Ghost.

Francis M. Lyman 25:61

In order for us to be prepared to do the will of God, and be in a position to build up His kingdom upon the earth, and to carry out His purposes, we must not only become united and act as the heart of one man, but we must obtain the Holy Spirit of God, and the mind and will of God concerning us, and be governed and controlled by it in all of our movements and acts, in order to be safe, and to secure unto ourselves salvation.

Wilford Woodruff 4:191

We cannot fulfill our engagements with the Almighty without we have that Spirit with us. We should so live as to acknowledge the Good Spirit continually. We cannot do this unless we let the Spirit of God rule in temporalities as well as in spiritual matters.

Daniel H. Wells 9:95

Our condition as a people is such that we cannot make the progress that is designed by God for us, unless we have His Spirit given unto us. We are assailed from many quarters. We have so much to contend with, that it requires the wisdom of God to direct us, and it requires His Holy Spirit constantly to be with us to enable us to perform our part in this great work.

George Q. Cannon 24:251

This is a great and important work — one that we do not fully comprehend. When the Spirit of the Lord rests powerfully upon us, we realize it to some extent; but we do not always have that Spirit in such copious measure, and when we are left to ourselves we are weak, frail and liable to err.

This shows to us that we should be more faithful than we have ever been, and that day and night, wherever we are and under whatever circumstances we may be placed, in order to enjoy the Spirit of the Gospel we must live to God by observing truth, honoring his law, and ever manifest a vigorous determination to accomplish the work he has assigned us.

Joseph F. Smith 11:309

No matter what the person is called to do, if it is to build up the kingdom of God on the earth, if he cheerfully performs the duty, he is entitled to the Spirit of the Lord — the Spirit of Truth — the Holy

Ghost; and will most assuredly possess the same. There is a time for preaching, for praying, for sacrament meetings, for labor, and when we are attending to any or all of these, in the season thereof, we are entitled to the purifying influence of the Spirit of God.

> Brigham Young 11:293
> See also 4:191-192 (next section); 24:236-237

Be Righteous

Pray without ceasing, and in everything give thanks. Is it not a hard task to live this religion without enjoying the spirit of it? Such a course worries the feelings, fills a person with sorrow and affliction, and makes him miserable.

The easiest life to live, by any mortal being on the earth, is to live in the light of God's countenance, and have fellowship with his Son Jesus Christ. I know this by my own experience. In this course there is no darkness, no sorrow, no grief. The power of the Spirit of God has preserved me in the vigour of youth, and I am as active as a boy.

How is it with you who do not enjoy the spirit of your religion? It is a hard life for you to live; and you had better, from this day, take a course to enjoy the Spirit of the Lord; then you will be numbered with the wise.

> Brigham Young 8:198

As I was remarking, unless we do obtain the Holy Spirit, we are in danger every step we take, we are not safe, neither are we in a condition to build up the kingdom of God or do His work.

I consider that the Lord requires this at the hand of every man and woman in Israel, every Latter-day Saint, that we first obtain the Holy Spirit, then bring forth the fruits of it unto salvation, then you will see this people keep their covenants and obey the commandments of God; this is the duty of all of us, and we should live our religion and follow its dictates.

When this is done, you will see this people awake and bring forth works of righteousness, then they will have faith, and they will have power, and rise up, and the power and glory of God will be made manifest through such instruments as the Lord has chosen in this dispensation upon the earth, into whose hands He has committed the Holy Priesthood.

> Wilford Woodruff 4:191-192
> See also 10:309; 13:8-9 (quoted in "Helps You to See Yourself As God Sees You" in Chapter 12); 16:38

Raise Our Children Properly

There is not a position that we can occupy in life, either as fathers, mothers, children, masters, servants, or as Elders of Israel holding the holy Priesthood in all its ramifications, but what we need continually is wisdom flowing from the Lord and intelligence communicated by him, that we may know how to perform correctly the various duties and avocations of life, and to fulfill the various responsibilities that rest upon us.

And hence the necessity all the day long, and every day, and every week, month, and year, and under all circumstances, of men leaning upon the Lord and being guided by that Spirit that flows from him, that we may not fall into error — that we may neither do anything wrong, say anything wrong, nor think anything wrong, and all the time retain that Spirit, which can only be kept by observing purity, holiness, and virtue, and living continually in obedience to the laws and commandments of God.

John Taylor 6:106

I say to fathers and mothers, never say a word that you would not be willing your son and daughter should say, or commit an act you would not sanction in your son or daughter, and so walk before your children that they may be prepared by your example to walk in the ways of life everlasting, and they will not depart from them.

And if they, notwithstanding your example, should become forward in their feelings, and unruly, they will soon see the folly of their ways and turn to their parents and acknowledge their faults and again wish to be feasted at their father's table.

Parents should never drive their children, but lead them along, giving them knowledge as their minds are prepared to receive it. Solomon has written, "He that spareth his rod hateth his son, but he that loveth him chasteneth him betimes." I do not think that these words of Solomon will justify the ruling of children with an iron hand. Chastening may be necessary betimes, but parents should govern their children by faith rather than by the rod, leading them kindly by good example into all truth and holiness.

Our children who are born in the Priesthood are legal heirs, and entitled to the revelations of the Lord, and as the Lord lives, his angels have charge over them, though they may be left to themselves occasionally.

We should learn our own nature, and live worthy of our being. When Jesus Christ was left to himself, in His darkest hour, he faltered not, but overcame. He was ordained to this work. . . .

At times our children may not be in possession of a good spirit, but if the parent continues to possess the good spirit, the children will have the bad spirit but a short time. Parents who are Latter-day Saints are the ruling power; they are the kings and queens. Rule in righteousness, and in the fear and love of God, and your children will follow you. May God bless you. Amen.

> Brigham Young 12:174

It is not possible for us as parents, to preside in our families, to set good examples before them, to set and keep our houses in order — as it is necessary they should be kept, that we may have salvation — unless we enjoy the Holy Ghost.

> Francis M. Lyman 25:61
>
> See also 21:46 (found in "Guide Us in Our Lives" at beginning of this chapter)

Help Us to Live the Celestial Law

Without this spirit, without revelation from the Most High, it is utterly impossible for the human family to be saved in the celestial kingdom of our Father and God.

> Orson Pratt 21:256-257

Now, can we live our religion unless we are in possession of the Holy Ghost all the time? We cannot. . . . No man can please the Lord God, only as he is dictated by the Holy Ghost; and he will not stay with you unless you keep in view the Father and the Son. . . . Are these principles the celestial law? I know no other. And how can you keep the celestial law without the Holy Ghost? You cannot. . . . Some may say, "How long will it be before the celestial law will be put into force?" Never, until you put it into force and execute it on yourselves.

> Heber C. Kimball 6:122

Accept and Follow the Prophet

I am not in the least fearful that any one will gain too much knowledge of God, and through that knowledge undertake to dictate me. If you know the Spirit of God, have the power of revelation, and know the mind of the Lord from day to day, I am not afraid of your disagreeing with me. Do not have any fears of knowing too much, lest you should feel to rise up and dictate me, as wives, in many cases, do their husbands.

> Brigham Young 8:66

Hence, for men spiritually unenlightened to be unable to comprehend the things of God is not peculiar to the dispensation in which we live, but it has been so in every age when God made known His will to the children of men.

Such individuals may come in contact with the greatest of Heaven's children and may associate with them day by day, and yet through not having that Spirit they will fail to recognize their nobility of character, and that they are divinely inspired.

Some of the members, even, of Jesus' own family, as we learn from the sacred record, ridiculed him; they could not recognize that their own brother, the son of their mother, was the Son of God, who was to die for the sins of the world; although they had been brought up with Jesus from childhood, they failed to recognize it for the very reason that Joseph Smith, and Brigham Young, and every prophet and apostle that ever lived on the face of the earth have not been recognized by many of their associates.

If their minds had been enlightened by the Spirit of God they would have recognized the men of God, and could have comprehended the things of God and the plan of salvation. . . . No man with his natural wisdom can comprehend the things of God; man never did do it and never can do it.

George Q. Cannon 11:334

Shall we not have confidence in God's Prophets, and in those whom He has placed to teach us? Those who are not satisfied with them are constantly grumbling and growling about their circumstances and the prosperity of the Church, but when we have the Holy Spirit, all is right, and we feel satisfied; the visions of the Almighty and of the heavens are before us night and day, and we have confidence in the holy Gospel, in the work of the Lord, in the Priesthood, and in those who hold that authority upon this earth.

Ezra T. Benson 3:63

See and Understand the Events of the Last Days

When I think upon the day and age in when [which] we live, when I think upon this day and dispensation in which the God of heaven has set His hand to carry out the fulfillment of the mighty prophecies contained within the lids of the Bible, the Old and New Testaments, the stick of Judah, I realize that in order to comprehend these things a man must be in possession of the Spirit of the Lord day by day.

Wilford Woodruff 24:237

But my experience has taught me that the Lord works in the midst of this people by natural means, and that the greatest events that have been spoken of by the Holy prophets will come along so naturally as the consequence of certain causes, that unless our eyes are enlightened by the Spirit of God, and the spirit of revelation rests [upon] us, we will fail to see that these are the events predicted by the holy prophets. . . .

And so with the great events that will take place in the future; they will come along in so natural a manner, the Lord will bring them to pass in such a way that they will not be accepted by the people, except by those who can comprehend the truth, as the fulfillment of predictions of the prophets. It requires the Spirit of God to enable men and women to understand the things of God; it requires the Spirit of God to enable the people to comprehend the work of God and to perceive his movements and providences among the children of men. The man who is destitute of the Spirit of God cannot comprehend the work of God. A woman whose mind has not been enlightened by that Spirit, cannot see or comprehend any of these events that take place in fulfillment of the prophecies of the holy prophets.

George Q. Cannon 21:267

The Holy Ghost reveals unto you things past, present, and to come; it makes your minds quick and vivid to understand the handy work of the Lord. Your joy is made full in beholding the footsteps of our Father going forth among the inhabitants of the earth; this is invisible to the world, but it is made visible to the Saints, and they behold the Lord in His providences, bringing forth the work of the last days.

Brigham Young 4:22

To Sustain Us

To know and to worship the true God, in the name of Jesus — in spirit and in truth — is the duty of man. To aid and qualify him for this service is the duty and office of the Holy Ghost. Man may fail through faltering and unfaithfulness, but the Spirit of God will never fail, nor abandon the faithful disciple.

Joseph F. Smith 19:191

10

Speaker and Hearer
Must Have the Spirit

The Need for the Spirit

But in our meetings, and in our teachings and instructions we need, today as much as we ever did, to be under the guidance and direction of the Almighty. There is no man living, and there never was a man living, who was capable of teaching the things of God only as he was taught, instructed and directed by the spirit of revelation proceeding from the Almighty.

And then there are no people competent to receive true intelligence, and to form a correct judgment in relation to the sacred principles of eternal life, unless they are under the influence of the same spirit, and hence speakers and hearers are all in the hands of the Almighty.

John Taylor 17:369

Preaching the word to Saint or sinner is of but little moment, unless there is a place in the hearts of the hearers to receive it; otherwise it is to them like sounding brass and a tinkling cymbal. To enjoy the light and power of the Holy Ghost day by day is prayed for by brother Pratt; but the preacher does not need it any more than the hearers. The preacher needs the power of the Holy Ghost to deal out to each heart a word in due season, and the hearers need the Holy Ghost to bring forth the fruits of the preached word of God to his glory.

Brigham Young 8:167

In arising to address you this morning, my brethren and sisters, I trust we shall have the presence and assistance of the Spirit of God, to lead our minds to those subjects that may be the most appropriate to you and to your circumstances. It is very desirable that we should have that Spirit to be with us, desirable both for the speaker and for the hearers, that our meeting may be mutually profitable. . . .

George Q. Cannon 24:251

See also 6:105-106; 8:306 (quoted in "Brings Happiness to You," chapter 12)

The Speaker's Responsibility

A.   Be Prepared

There are many, perhaps, who feel a disposition to neglect all improvement of mind, thinking that if they are placed in a position where they are called upon to preach, God will give them, not only the subject, but the language also, and everything pertaining to the duties of their callings as public speakers.

Although we are taught that we are to take no thought beforehand what we shall say, yet we are nowhere taught in the revelations of God to let our minds run down — our understandings and our judgment to be spent in idleness, without treasuring up the things of the kingdom of God, and storing up useful knowledge. Indeed, we are commanded in the revelations of the Most High directly to the contrary from the idea which has prevailed among some.

Orson Pratt 7:74-75

Nevertheless, the servants of God are instructed to "treasure up in their hearts continually the words of life," with the promise that if they do this and are diligent in seeking for the mind and will of God, in the very hour that they are needed words shall be placed in their mouths, or ideas be brought up in their minds, which shall be for the benefit of all who hear.

Charles W. Penrose 21:220

B.   Keep It Simple

Now when we present ourselves to a congregation of people, the first thing should be plainly and simply to communicate to them the first principles that we receive, in the best possible manner. But what is the best way to communicate them to the inhabitants of the earth? . . .

The best method is to select the best and simplest way in our possession, and you will find that to be the most successful method of proclaiming the Gospel. You may note it when you will, in men that go forth to proclaim the truth, and you discover that the man who has the fewest words communicates his ideas to the people, as a general thing, in the plainest manner. . . .

It is my advice that our Elders should study brevity in all their discourses and communications to the people, and that they should speak in the plainest and simplest manner; for if they were to do this — speak so that the unlearned can comprehend, then the learned will be sure to understand.

George A. Smith 3:24

C.   Teach by the Holy Ghost

I would be glad, when I speak to the people, that the Lord would let His Holy Spirit accompany my words, for I do not want my words to go alone. We have to speak to this people often, and when we talk to them like a man reading off a sermon that is written, it takes but little effect. When words go to the people alone, they are not profited by them.

Jedediah M. Grant 4:73

I have, through upwards of forty years' experience in the public ministry, learned some few lessons in regard to public speaking. In the first place I know that the wisdom of man avails but very little, and that our own judgement, thoughts and reflections are not what the Lord requires; but he does require, and has required, ever since the rise of this Church, that his servants should speak by the power of the Holy Ghost.

A revelation given to the Elders of this Church in the year 1831, says, "My servants shall be sent forth to the east and to the west, and to the north and to the south, and they shall lift up their voices and speak and prophesy, as seemeth me good; but if you receive not the Spirit you shall not teach." This is a commandment that the Lord gave to his servants over forty years ago. I have seen a few times from the commencement of my ministry, when my mind seemed to be entirely closed up, and when what few words I could stammer forth before a congregation, were altogether unsatisfactory to my own mind, and I presume to those who heard me.

But I do feel thankful to God that latterly, from year to year, he has favored me with a liberty of utterance and with the power and gift of the Holy Ghost. I acknowledge his hand in this, for I know it has come from him, and having experienced the two conditions of mind I know the difference.

Orson Pratt 15:229

I speak these things because they come to my mind. When I arise to speak, I have never a premeditated subject; I let God, by the Holy Ghost, dictate me and control me, just as a musician would his violin. It is the player on the instrument that plays the tune; the instrument does not dictate the player. So I should be in the hands of God, to be dictated by him; for we are told that the Holy Ghost, the Comforter, will teach us all things past, present, and to come.

The Holy Ghost knows the minds of this people, and what is necessary to deal out to every man and every woman in due season — their portion. If I am not dictated by the Holy Ghost, I cannot communicate to you that which is necessary.

Heber C. Kimball 5:172

When the time should come for His servants to address the people, He would give unto them the very things that were needed. How do I know, how does any other man in this congregation know the thoughts and the fears and the wants of you who are here today? There may be souls here hungering for the word of God, tried and tempted in many directions, annoyed and perplexed with the cares of life and with those anxieties that are connected with our earthly existence. Who shall tell these souls that which they need?

Can any man out of his own wisdom, from the depths of his own thoughts, give the needed strength and comfort to those hungry souls? It is impossible. God must do it. God must pour out His Holy Spirit. God must help as he has promised to do, and we His children must put ourselves in a position to be helped so that we can claim the blessing.

George Q. Cannon 24:179-180
See Also 3:7

The Hearer's Needs

It is often remarked that we do not understand things alike, but I am of the opinion that the inhabitants of the earth understand in the spirit, or, in other words, in the intelligent portion of their organisms, nearer alike than they have power to communicate.

We believe we are entitled to the gift of the Holy Ghost in extent according to the discretion and wisdom of God and our faithfulness; which gift brings all things to our remembrance, past, present, and to come, that are necessary for us to know, and as far as our minds are prepared to receive the knowledge of God revealed by that all-wise Agent. The Holy Ghost is God's minister, and is delegated to visit the sons and daughters of men. All intelligent beings pertaining to this earth are instructed from the same source. . . .

He also gives intelligence by angels, as well as by the inspiration of the Holy Spirit, and by opening the minds of the Saints to behold in vision things as they are in eternity. When true doctrines are advanced, though they may be new to the hearers, yet the principles contained in them are perfectly natural and easy to be understood, so much so that the hearers often imagine that they had always known them. This arises from the influence of the Spirit of Truth upon the spirit of intelligence that is within each person.

The influence that comes from heaven is all the time teaching the children of men, "There is a spirit in man, and the inspiration of the Almighty giveth them understanding." Again, "The spirit of man is the candle of the Lord, searching all the inward parts of the belly." Again, "How oft is the candle of the wicked put out."

We have nothing independent of the Almighty. We preach, we hear, and we are instructed. We try to so live as to gain more information, more light, more command over ourselves, and more influence and power to increase the good and discourage the evil, until we can comprehend the great principles of existence and eternal progression.

Brigham Young 9:254

I do not know of any way whereby we can be taught, instructed and be made to comprehend our true position, only by being under the influence of the Spirit of the living God. A man may speak by the Spirit of God, but it requires a portion of that Spirit also in those who hear, to enable them to comprehend correctly the importance of the things that are delivered to them and hence the difficulty the Lord and his Saints have always had in making the people comprehend the things that are especially for their interests.

We all consider that if we could be taught of God it would be very well; I suppose the world generally would consider it to be a great blessing. Then the question arises in their minds, whether the teachings they receive come from God or not. How are they to know that? I know of no other way than that which is spoken in the Scriptures, "There is a spirit in man, and the inspiration of the Almighty giveth it understanding." And, again, we are told in the New Testament, that "No man knoweth the things of God but by the Spirit of God."

Hence all the wisdom, all the intelligence, all the reasoning, all the philosophy and all the arguments that could be brought to bear on the human mind would be of no avail unless the mind of man is prepared to receive this teaching — prepared by the Spirit of the Lord, the same Spirit which conveys the intelligence.

John Taylor 10:145
See also 8:130

The Need for the Spirit in Our Meetings

A. Our Responsibility

If any of you feel that there is no life in your meetings, as I occasionally hear some of the brethren say, then it becomes your duty to go and instill life into that meeting, and do your part to produce an increase of the Spirit and power of God in the meetings in your locality. If there is a fast meeting, or prayer meeting, why not somebody in that district go filled with the spirit and power of God, and assist to encourage, instruct, comfort and edify the Saints?

I have been an Elder in this Church for years, and I have been accustomed to teach every man and woman the duties enjoined upon them by the law of Christ; and when there was not a good spirit in a meeting, I have endeavored to instill one, and did not ask for any permission to do so. I want the Elders to be filled with the spirit of teaching, and I want each and every one of us to so live as to obtain our share of it, and to have the influence of the Spirit of the Lord to dictate to us. If these my brethren will live and act according to the Priesthood that is upon them, the Lord will be satisfied, and so will his servants.

Brigham Young 10:309

Language is too frail to express the rich sentiments of the hearts of the Saints; the tongue fails to utter the glory and the pleasures of the kingdom of God. It cannot do it; language fails. There is a display of the Holy Spirit in the understanding that surpasses all language; it cannot be told; it is past being told or described. This is right; it is as it should be, for language is poor: the best we know of is poor.

I am not precisely like some of our Elders who think that unless somebody is talking all the time, nobody can be edified. It is true that we come together to be edified by hearing each other speak: but when a body of people come together, that body should bring the agency of the Holy Spirit with them; and I drink of the fountain of intelligence, whether anybody speaks or not.

Joseph Young 6:206

B. The Need for Order

[President Heber C. Kimball interrupted a talk by Wilford Woodruff in the Salt Lake Tabernacle to say:]

Shut that door and let it remain so, for I tell you there is no one can enjoy the peaceful influence of the Holy Spirit where there is confusion; and I am sure this congregation cannot while that door is going clickitty-clack.

Heber C. Kimball 4:191

C. The Spiritual Results

Persons know and will continue to know and understand many things by the manifestations of the Spirit, that through the organization of the tabernacle it is impossible otherwise to convey. Much of the most important information is alone derived through the power and testimony of the Holy Ghost in the speaker, revealing itself to the understanding and spirit of the hearer. This is the only way you can convey a knowledge of the invisible things of God.

Brigham Young 8:41

The Book of Mormon tells us, that the angels speak by the power of the Holy Ghost, and man when under the influence of it, speaks the language of angels. Why does he speak in this language? Because the Holy Ghost suggests the ideas which he speaks; and it gives him utterance to convey them to the people.

Orson Pratt 3:101

I feel thankful to meet with the Latter-day Saints in this house to participate in the enjoyment of this Conference: for it is really enjoyment to me to listen to the instructions imparted to the Saints by the power of the Holy Ghost through the covenants of God. It is not supposed that when we come together as we do this morning, that we wish to be treated to the views and opinions of men.

The Lord has instructed his servants to speak as they are moved upon by the Holy Ghost, and it has been shown to us that it is our privilege when we assemble on such occasions to receive instructions, not in the enticing words of man's wisdom, but in the demonstration and power of the Holy Ghost; and this will be the case when we assemble in the right way and unite our faith and our attention and our spiritual energy so as to call down upon us the blessings of the Almighty, and to have the presence of those influences, those ministering spirits who are sent forth to minister to the heirs of salvation.

It is our privilege in these public gatherings appointed for the worship of God, to have the presence of these holy ones in our midst, and to have the power of the Almighty to rest upon both speaker and hearer, that we may be fed and nourished by the bread of life that comes down from heaven, and that when we part and go to our respective callings and places of abode we may each carry with us "a live coal from the altar."

Charles W. Penrose 21:45

11

Missionaries Need
the Holy Ghost

It is exceedingly interesting to me, as I have no doubt it is to all Latter-day Saints, to hear the Elders who have been on missions bear a faithful testimony, on their return, to the truth of the work in which they have been engaged.

It is a tolerably easy matter to tell, in listening to them speaking, whether they have been faithful or not in magnifying their Priesthood and calling, for a man who does not magnify his Priesthood, and who is not faithful in the discharge of the duties entrusted to him, generally manifests it by the spirit which he possesses and with which he speaks.

And so, also, when men have been faithful and have striven to magnify their calling, a spirit and influence attend them that bear testimony of their faithfulness. No man can go out, ordained by those who have the authority, in faith and in humility to preach the principles of the everlasting Gospel, however peculiar and difficult the circumstances may be that surround him, however great the trials and the persecutions that he may have to contend with, without receiving an unction from the Holy One, that will bear testimony to him that the work in which he is engaged is of God, and that he has been called of God to declare the principles of life and salvation unto the people among whom his lot may be cast.

There is this peculiarity and influence about this work, there is the demonstration of the Holy Ghost, which descends with convincing and overwhelming power upon all those who place themselves in a position to receive it; and there is no labor under the sun, I care not what it may be, or how pleasant the circumstances that surround him, at all comparable with the labor of an Elder in this Church, who endeavors, in humility and meekness, to magnify his calling.

There is no joy which a human soul is capable of comprehending, that approaches the delight and the satisfaction which laboring in the ministry of the Son of God confers upon him who does so in faithfulness.

He may be destitute, he may be without purse and scrip, as our Elders travel, he may be in the midst of enemies, he may be haled to prison, and treated with contumely, and have all manner of evil heaped upon him; but if he is faithful to God, if he is faithful to his Priesthood, and magnifies it to the extent of his ability, there is a power, an influence, and a joy resting upon and accompanying him, and filling him from the crown of his head to the soles of his feet, that are incomprehensible to those who have not experienced them.

And for such a man to doubt that God is with him, and that the work he is engaged in is the work of God, would be as difficult as to doubt that the sun's rays ever beam upon him, or that there is no warmth or light connected with them; in fact, such a man could as easily doubt his own existence, and the testimony of every sense that he possesses, as to doubt the testimony of God which rests down upon him.

George Q. Cannon 18:82-83

Teach by the Spirit

What Elders have been successful? The men that have stood before the people, and by the power of the Holy Ghost have declared the word of the Lord God to them; and here let me say in this connection, there never was a congregation that listened to a discourse delivered by an Elder of Israel, and that discourse was delivered by the power and demonstration and Spirit of the Almighty, but there came to every man and woman in that congregation a response by that same Spirit, "that is true."

It bore testimony there and then to the truth of the remarks of the servant of God, and by this means, and by this means only will those who reject the truth stand condemned before God in the day that they will appear before Him to give an account of their acts in this life.

Joseph E. Taylor 23:244

But the inquiry arises in my mind, Do the Elders realize the importance of their missions? Do they realize that in their administration they carry with them the keys of life and death, not pertaining to this life alone, but to this in connection with all the life there is?

It is necessary that you should fully realize this in your calling as
Elders in the Church of Jesus Christ. The thousands and tens of
thousands of incidents that make up the sum of human lives, whether
for good or evil, depend on a momentary watchfulness and care.

If an Elder, in preaching the Gospel, does not feel that he has the
power to preach life and salvation, and to legally administer the
ordinances, and that, too, by the power of God, he will not fill his
mission to his own credit, nor to the good of the people, and the
advancement and honour of the kingdom of God. From all I can read,
from all I can gather from the revelations from God to man, and from
the revelations of the Spirit to me, no man can successfully preach the
Gospel and be owned, blessed, and acknowledged by the heavens,
unless he preaches by the power of God through direct revelation.

Not but that, in a great many instances, a man may not be
manifestly under the immediate and powerful influences and direction
of revelation to dictate him all the time in his meditations and
reasonings, and yet can advance many good ideas that he has gathered
by means of his natural reasoning. But to magnify and make
honourable the calling of an Elder of this Church, I cannot conceive, in
my understanding, any other true principle by which it can be done,
only when perfectly controlled by the Spirit of the Lord.

When men enjoy the spirit of their missions and realize their calling
and standing before the Lord and the people, it constitutes the happiest
portions of their lives. . . .

But let one go forth who is careful to logically prove all he says by
numerous quotations from the revelations, and let another travel with
him who can say, by the power of the Holy Ghost, Thus saith the Lord,
and tell what the people should believe — what they should do — how
they should live, and teach them to yield to the principles of salvation
— though he may not be capable of producing a single logical
argument — though he may tremble under a sense of his weakness,
cleaving to the Lord for strength, as such men generally do, you will
invariably find that the man who testifies by the power of the Holy
Ghost will convince and gather many more of the honest and upright
than will the merely logical reasoner.

Debate and argument have not that saving effect that has testifying
to the truth as the Lord reveals it to the Elder by the Spirit. I think you
will all agree with me in this; at least, such is my experience.

I do not wish to be understood as throwing a straw in the way of the
Elders' storing their minds with all the arguments they can gather to
urge in defense of their religion, nor do I wish to hinder them in the

least from learning all they can with regard to religions and governments. The more knowledge the Elders have the better.

It is well to perfectly understand the religious and governmental theories of the world; it is satisfactory: yet, in preaching the Gospel, an Elder who prides himself in using good sound arguments and logic is not so apt to lean upon the Lord for his Spirit as are those who are not so particularly gifted in reasoning.

It is our duty, so far as we can, to gain knowledge and information pertaining to human life and the organization of the kingdoms, thrones, empires, and republics of the earth — to become well acquainted with their religions, laws, manners of administration, pursuits of life, manufactures, agriculture, arts, manners and customs, etc: but when we are possessed of all this knowledge, we need the power of God to teach the truths of the holy Gospel. I wish you to bear this truth in your memories and put it in practice.

Brigham Young 8:52-54

When we go forth as the servants of God, we are dictated by the Holy Ghost, and the Holy Ghost will speak the truth, and that is the word of God, it is the revelations of Jesus Christ, and it is the voice of God to us.

Heber C. Kimball 2:221

If you wish to know why the simple testimony of the humble servants of God gathers together this people from the nations of the earth, it is because there was place found in their hearts for the word.

When I went to Denmark, I could not speak the first word of their language, or know the first letter of their alphabet. I was to all intents and purposes a barbarian to them, and they were barbarians to me. I went there because I was sent, with an intention to do the best I knew how, as the Spirit of the Lord might direct me. You may ask if I received the gift of tongues, that I could begin and speak to them in their own language by the power of the Holy Ghost without studying. I answer, Yes, when it pleased the Lord to give it to me; and when it did not, I remained silent. I did not have any special anxiety to preach to them in their own tongue any more than the Lord wanted me to do.

I did not do a great deal of preaching in that country, but I did whatever the Lord put into my heart to do as near as I knew how; and I learned the language as fast as the Spirit of the Lord enabled me to do so, that I might bear my testimony to them in their own tongue, and that I might understand what they said to me when they asked me questions and required explanations; and when they wished to correspond with me, that I might be able to write an answer.

I had to learn to read and write, and talk to them in their own language. Did the Spirit of the Lord assist me? Yes. I learned their language and became so familiar with it as to write and speak with them in six months' time.

The Holy Ghost was with me to assist me. In twenty-one months I published the Book of Mormon, the Book of Doctrine and Covenants, and the Hymn Book, and eight or ten pamphlets. . . .

I was there comparatively alone, and the harvest great and the labourers few, and the Spirit bore testimony that the Lord had much people there. I saw, if they were all to be sought out and gathered home by the labours of men sent from America, and after travelling so long a journey to learn their language, that it was a great work; and the words of Alma came forcibly to my mind, that the Lord raises up men among all the nations of the earth, to give them that portion of his word which they are capable of receiving.

And I cried unto the Lord, saying, "O Lord, raise up labourers and send them into this harvest — men of their own tongue, who have been raised among them and are familiar with the spirits of the people. He has done it. Before I left, there was quite a little army of Elders and Priests, Teachers and Deacons, labouring in the vineyard; and thousands have rejoiced in the testimony of the Gospel borne to them by their fellow-countrymen. . . .

We testify and bear witness that it is not of man, but of God — that it is the power of the Gospel of Jesus Christ — that it is the gift and influence of the Holy Ghost that bears witness to the hearts of this people. When in the simplicity of my heart I could speak but little unto them with stammering lips, I said more with my eyes and fingers than with my tongue. The power of the Holy Ghost rested upon the people; and when I asked them if they understood me, "Yes," said they, "we understood it all."

It was not because I spoke it fully with my tongue, but God made them understand me. If I asked them if they believed it, "Yes," would be the reply; "we have the testimony of the Holy Ghost bearing witness within us that it is true."

I laid my hands upon the men that were raised up around me, and sent them to preach the Gospel; and they were just such men as the Lord sent me; no matter if they were shoemakers, carpenters, chimney-sweepers, or any other kind of trade. I told them to go forth and bear witness of what they had heard, and of what they knew; and every time they opened their mouth, a stream of light would flow from them to the people, who were melted before them. This is the experience of every man of God upon all the earth.

Erastus Snow 7:128-129

Instructions for Missionaries on How to Have the Holy Ghost

I wish to say a few words to the missionaries — to those who are going abroad to preach the Gospel of Christ. I want to give you a word of exhortation and counsel, brethren: that is, whenever you are in doubt about any duty or work which you have to perform, never proceed to do anything until you go and labour in prayer and get the Holy Spirit. Wherever the Spirit dictates you to go or to do, that will be right; and, by following its dictates, you will come out right.

We shall be brought to many places during our career in the ministry among the nations of the earth, where we may consider a certain course of procedure to be right; but, if we do not know, it will be better for us to go before the Lord, and ask in faith that we may be instructed in the way of life.

I will take the liberty of saying that it is your privilege, brethren, to get the mind and will of the Lord in relation to your duties while abroad among the people; and it is also the privilege of the whole people who are called Israel to obtain the revelations of the Holy Spirit to guide them in every duty in life. Whatever position a man may stand in, it is his privilege, as a Saint of God, to enjoy this blessing; and a man who understands himself will not move without the operations of that Spirit to lead him.

Wilford Woodruff 5:85

We say to them, Go forth and preach the Gospel, gain an experience, learn wisdom, and walk humbly before your God, that you may receive the Holy Ghost to guide and direct you, and teach you all things past, present, and to come. I cannot say that this is sufficient to say to them, for it is not. . . .

Those Elders about to start on their missions will declare before this congregation and before the whole world that they do know, by the power of God, that Joseph Smith is a true Prophet of God, and that this is the work of God; that God has set his hand to gather Israel: but let them neglect their duty and get into darkness, and they will lose this Spirit and testimony. They do not see this with their natural eyes, for it is spiritually discerned, as all things of God are.

Let them do wrong and lose the Spirit, and by-and-by they apostatize and declare that they do not know "Mormonism" to be true, and think they never did. How many are there of this class? Brethren, live your religion. As a mischievous child needs constant watching to keep it from falling into the fire, or otherwise injuring itself, so you need watching, warning, teaching, and admonishing all the time; you need to be continually teased to your duty.

Brigham Young 8:176-177

Never, through committing evil, lay the foundation for a person to truthfully speak evil of you. If you pursue this course, you will be justified before God, Jesus, angels, and your brethren. You can then testify to the truth, and teach it in all plainness, simplicity, and honesty, and be able to bid defiance to the world.

In your traveling you will have to trust in the Lord. I do not know whether you have means sufficient to enable you to go directly to your fields of labour. Probably some of you have, and some have not. Strive to be full of the Holy Ghost, and the necessary means will come to you, often in a way you cannot comprehend, and you will be expedited in your journeyings and perform your missions.

And furthermore, if you will not drop one thread in the garments of your characters, from the time you leave here, I am not in the least doubtful in my mind — I have not a shade of hesitancy in my feelings in promising that each of you will accomplish a mission that will please our Father in heaven and every good person on the earth and in heaven, and live to return to this place.

Have faith to live, and do just as you should do; and do not imagine that you can go to the right or to the left, or do this, that, or the other wrong with impunity, thinking that it will be well enough in the end. Do that alone which you know to be right and which you ought to do. When you come to that which you do not know to be right, let it alone and trust in the Lord, and you will live. . . .

When you reach your fields of labour, do the best you can; and when the enemy comes along and tells you that you are somebody, say, "Mr. Devil, it is none of your business. What I have spoken is what the Lord gave to me. I have presented it to the people, and that is all I have to do with it."

If you cannot preach as nicely and smoothly as you wish, and a feeling rises that you cannot preach at all — that you had better return home, tell Satan to get behind you — that he has no power to dictate whether you preach a word or not, for you are in the Lord's service. So live that the Spirit of the Lord can instruct your minds at all times, and you can then defy the Devil and all his emissaries. If you have nothing from the Lord to present to the people, be as willing to be silent as you would to preach what might be termed a splendid discourse. . . .

Some of our Missionaries, after an absence of two or three years, return with their eyes cast down: their countenances are fallen. I wish you to take such a course that you can come home with your heads up. Keep yourselves clean, from the crowns of your heads to the soles of your feet; be pure in heart — otherwise you will return bowed down in spirit and with a fallen countenance, and will feel as though you never could rise again.

When the Quorum of the Twelve was first organized, Joseph said that the Elders of Israel, and particularly the Twelve Apostles, would receive more temptations, be more buffetted, and have greater difficulty to escape the evil thrown in their way by females than by any other means.

This is one of Satan's most powerful auxiliaries with which to weaken the influence of the ministers of Christ, and bring them down from their high position and calling into darkness, shame, and disgrace. You will have to guard more strictly against that than against any other evil that may beset you. Make up your minds not to yield, for one moment, to the subtle insinuations of the animal propensities of your natures while you are absent on the Lord's errands. Rather, suffer your heads to be taken from your shoulders than to sacrifice your honour, violate your covenants, and forfeit the sacred trust reposed in you. . . .

I do not think there was worse said about the Savior and his disciples in ancient days than has been said about the people of Utah in modern times. Take no notice of this, but attend to the business about which you have been sent. Tell this generation the truth, and pass along.

Many will tell you that your religion is all error. Reply that you will make an exchange with them of ten errors for one truth. Do not contend or argue much, but pass along peaceably and preach the first principles of the Gospel — faith in God and his Son Jesus Christ, and teach the people to repent of their sins and be baptized for the remission of them, and they shall receive the gift of the Holy Ghost through the laying on of the hands of the Elders.

It is often the case that some wish to preach about things of which they have little or no knowledge. Let alone that which you do not know or most assuredly believe to be true — doctrines which you do not perfectly understand, and strive to be honest.

If you do not understand a doctrine or a portion of Scripture, when information is asked of you, say that the Lord has not revealed that to you, or that he has not opened your understanding to grasp it, and that you do not feel safe in giving an interpretation until he does. May God bless you! Amen.

Brigham Young 8:54-56

This Spirit animates our young brethren when faithfully attending to their duties while on missions, and it is this which enables them to say that the time so spent has been the happiest of their lives.

This enables our Elders, many of whom are to a great degree destitute of education, to stand before the learned, wise and noble, and the divines of the day, and declare the principles of the Gospel of Jesus. Who could do this under such circumstances without the Spirit of the Lord? I do not know the individual; and if there be those who could they are such as I referred to at the commencement of my remarks who, destitute of a knowledge of their own weakness, can stand up anywhere and speak with boldness, and exhibit themselves, whether it be wisdom or folly to do so.

None but those who enjoy the Spirit of the Lord, who are filled with the Holy Ghost, can stand before emperors, kings and wise men of the earth and speak the words of truth with all that simplicity and pleasure that children converse together [with]. . . .

I recollect when I left, to go to England, I was unable to walk twenty rods without assistance. I was helped to the edge of the river Mississippi and carried across. When brother Kimball and I started on our journey there was a struggle between us and the powers of earth and hell whether or not we should accomplish our mission.

We were in the depths of poverty, caused by being driven from Missouri, where we had left all. I recollect that one of my own sisters pitied my condition and situation; she was sorry for me, and said, "Brother Brigham, what necessity is there for you to go to England while you were sick? Why not tarry here until you are well?" I said to her, as I started off one morning, "Sister Fanny, I never felt better in my life."

She was a very eccentric woman and, looking at me, with tears in her eyes, she said, "You lie." I said nothing, but I was determined to go to England or to die trying. My firm resolve was that I would do what I was required to do in the Gospel of life and salvation, or I would die trying to do it. I am so today.

Brigham Young 13:211

Promises to Missionaries Who Have the Holy Ghost

You are to claim blessings by your conduct, you are so instructed;

some are apt to be so neglectful and remiss in their duties that they are not able to claim them. They forget what is in store for them, and do not pray for the Spirit to impress those blessings upon their minds, but suffer their minds to be drawn out too much upon temporal business instead of the things of God, and become weary in mind and body, so that they feel like neglecting the more prominent duties, such as family prayer and many others.

This is because they do not enjoy sufficient of the Spirit of the Lord, for it is able to strengthen every one of you. Look at the promises made to the missionaries, "He that shall go forth to preach the Gospel without purse or scrip shall not be weary, nor darkened in spirit nor in body."

What is it that strengthens them so that they do not become weary in body and mind? The Elders abroad are called upon to labor diligently, and many times to sit up almost all night to teach the pure principles of eternal life, and when they lie down they rest perfectly calm as though they were not weary, and arise invigorated with faith, intelligence, and power; their minds and bodies are strengthened by the power of God.

Orson Pratt 3:349-350

Missionaries have been called. If they go and magnify their callings, they will be filled with the testimony that has been so freely manifested during our Conference; they will be filled with the Holy Ghost, and be able to bear testimony of the truths of the Gospel. It may be apparently in weakness. They may consider it so themselves. Their language may be feeble, their words feebly uttered, their sentences broken; but, after all, it will be the power of God unto this generation.

If you Missionaries will seek for the testimony of the Holy Ghost to go with you — if you will seek diligently for the power of God to accompany you, you need not be afraid of the nations; for your testimony will condemn the people who reject it, and it will save all those who receive it.

Orson Pratt 8:48

The Elders who have faithfully fulfilled their missions, warning all men who came within the sound of their voices, have identified themselves with the Savior, and with the Father, and with the Holy Ghost; and the Holy Ghost will abide with all such if they continue faithful; and herein consists the authority and power of every faithful servant of God in this and in all ages of the world.

Heber C. Kimball 11:145

But get the Holy Ghost and you have a testimony that cannot

deceive you. It never deceived any man, and it never will. It is by this power and principle that the Elders of Israel have been sustained from the first day they commenced their labors until today.

Wilford Woodruff 16:38

The most ignorant of our Elders, with the Spirit and power of God upon them, can, in knowledge of Scripture, lead the smartest of the Gentile priests into deep water, and dip them under, and draw them back again at their pleasure, and confound the Scripture knowledge of the priestcraft that is on the earth.

Brigham Young 8:198

See also 11:135 (chapter 12, "Helps You Understand Your Priesthood Duties"); 15:285 (chapter 12, "Builds Brotherly Consideration for Others"); 19:20 (chapter 12, "Bears Testimony to Us"); 23:17 (chapter 12, "Enables You to Teach Others and Testify to Them")

——— 12 ———

What the Holy Ghost
Will Do for You

Will Teach You the Things of God

The Holy Ghost takes of the Father, and of the Son, and shows it to the disciples. It shows them things past, present, and to come. It opens the vision of the mind, unlocks the treasures of wisdom, and they begin to understand the things of God; their minds are exalted on high; their conceptions of God and His creations are dignified, and "Hallelujah to God and the Lamb in the highest," is the constant language of their hearts.

They comprehend themselves and the great object of their existence. They also comprehend the designs of the wicked one, and the designs of those who serve him; they comprehend the designs of the Almighty in forming the earth, and mankind upon it, and the ultimate purpose of all His creations. It leads them to drink at the fountain of eternal wisdom, justice, and truth; they grow in grace, and in the knowledge of the truth as it is in Jesus Christ, until they see as they are seen, and know as they are known.

Brigham Young 1:241

There are many things that we can learn, already within our reach, without any special and direct revelation, that is, when I say special revelation, I mean without the Lord revealing directly by a vision, the ministration of an angel, or by direct words, as he revealed many things to the ancient revelators, seers, and Prophets.

There are a great many things that we can learn independently of these direct revelations; but still we need the help of the Lord, in some measure, in our researches, to learn anything; we need the influence of

the Spirit of God to quicken the light that is within us, for light cleaves to light, and the Spirit of God is light, and it cleaves unto the light that enters into the composition of the spirit of man; and when we keep his commandments the Lord is ever ready and willing to quicken the judgment, inform the mind, and lead us along in our thinking and reflecting powers, that we may have power to understand a great many truths, without his coming out and saying, — "Thus saith the Lord."
Orson Pratt 17:327

We believe that it is necessary for man to be placed in communication with God; that he should have revelation from him, and that unless he is placed under the influence of the inspiration of the Holy Spirit, he can know nothing about the things of God.

I do not care how learned a man may be, or how extensively he may have traveled; I do not care what his talent, intellect or genius may be, at what college he may have studied, how comprehensive his views or what his judgment may be on other matters, he cannot understand certain things without the Spirit of God, and that necessarily introduces the principle I before referred to — the necessity of revelation.

Not revelation in former times, but present and immediate revelation, which shall lead and guide those who possess it in all the paths of life here, and to eternal life hereafter.... Whoever heard of true religion without communication with God?
John Taylor 16:371

The Spirit may rest upon many and reveal to them the wonderful things of God; but when it does it will prompt them to obey the commands of the Lord Jesus. Is this the fact? It is.

Well, we will say it is very fortunate for those who receive this Gospel and the spirit of it in their hearts, for it awakes within them a desire to know and understand the things of God more than they ever did before in their lives, and they begin to inquire, read and search, and when they go to the Father in the name of Jesus he will not leave them without a witness.
Brigham Young 14:135

As the light that comes from the sun reveals through our natural eyes those objects which we see around us, so the Holy Ghost coming from God opens up and makes clear and plain the things of eternity, those things that are called spiritual, although they are all spiritual to our Heavenly Father.
Charles W. Penrose 25:40-41

See also 3:144-145; 4:227; 6:105-106, 166; 8:41, 130, 183; 10:145, 216;

11:333; 18:199 (see "Places Us in Communion with God," this chapter); 19:91, 366; 22:84-85 (quoted in chapter 3)

Reveals Knowledge to You

It takes of the things of the Father and makes them plain to the human mind; it makes things past clear to the understanding of man, and it lifts up the curtain of futurity and shows things to come. It is the Spirit of prophecy, the testimony of Jesus; it is the light of God to the human soul.

And as natural light discloses to the vision of men the objects of the material universe, without which none can discern them, so the Holy Ghost is the light of God which reveals to the spirits of men the things of eternal life, and without which men cannot understand the things of God.

>Charles W. Penrose 20:217

This spirit, when received, and when we give it our attention, and bring our minds to bear upon the object of its operations, is calculated to instruct and impart much information and knowledge to both male and female who are in the possession of it. The Spirit of God is a spirit of revelation. It always was a spirit that revealed something to the human family, when mankind were in possession of it.

Without this spirit, without revelation from the Most High, it is utterly impossible for the human family to be saved in the celestial kingdom of our Father and God.

>Orson Pratt 21:256-257

But the man filled with the Holy Ghost has got the advantage of students who graduate at our universities. Why? Because he can learn more in ten minutes, in regards to many things, than another, not so favored, can in all his life.

Indeed, he can learn some things by the operations of the Holy Ghost, which no natural man or woman could learn, however gifted they may be. You may inquire where they could learn these things? I answer, by the revelations of the Holy Ghost, which brings to light many things that are past, and shows things that are in the future.

The Lord is just as able to show one of his pupils, who will take the necessary steps to be taught, what will take place a year, or ten years, or a hundred, or a thousand or more years hence, as the principals in our universities are to teach persons concerning things present.

God is not confined to the present, or to things immediately concerning his pupils, or those who may enter into the university he has prepared, but he opens the past and future to the minds of men, just as Jesus promised his disciples, when he was about to leave them. "Howbeit when he, the Spirit of Truth, is come, he will guide you into all truth; and he will show you things to come."

Orson Pratt 19:284
See also 2:346; 6:105-106; 17:369

Will Teach You the Purpose of Life

When the Spirit of revelation from God inspires a man, his mind is opened to behold the beauty, order, and glory of the creation of this earth and its inhabitants, the object of its creation, and the purpose of its creator in peopling it with his children.

He can then clearly understand that our existence here is for the sole purpose of exaltation and restoration to the presence of our Father and God, where we may progress endlessly in the power of godliness. After the mind has thus been illuminated, the ignorance and blindness of the great mass of mankind are more apparent.

Brigham Young 9:256

Will Enlarge Your Mind

Man possesses a spirit that must endure forever — a spirit that comes from God; and inasmuch as he is not fed from the same source or power that created him, he is not and cannot be satisfied. . . . But in these days, when the holy Priesthood is restored to us, we have no excuse for saying that our minds are not satisfied, for the blessings are given to us; they are within our reach, and it is your privilege and mine to enjoy them.

Wilford Woodruff 8:268-269

Many a soul may be drooping for the want of a spiritual moisture, and they do not know what the difficulty is. There are obstacles in the way that need removing, that our minds may be enlightened by the light of the Spirit of the living God.

Daniel H. Wells 12:234

The principles of eternal life are manifested unto us by the inspiration of the Holy Ghost; for that Spirit rests upon us — it influences our minds; and if we watch those teachings, having within us the right feeling, we shall comprehend things clearly as they are.

Wilford Woodruff 9:56-57

The Holy Ghost reveals unto you things past, present, and to come; it makes your minds quick and vivid to understand the handy work of the Lord. Your joy is made full in beholding the footsteps of our Father going forth among the inhabitants of the earth; this is invisible to the world, but it is made visible to the Saints, and they behold the Lord in His providences, bringing forth the work of the last days.

Brigham Young 4:22
See also 21:220

Brings Knowledge Back to Your Mind

It will teach you all things; it will bring to your remembrance past things that you have forgotten, things that are now present, and show you the providences of God, the dealings of the Lord with his people, his designs in organizing the world and in peopling it, etc. You Latter-day Saints, live humbly and live your religion faithfully, that you may enjoy the spirit of revelation to a fullness. . . .

You will receive a Spirit that will bring all things to your remembrance, past, present, and to come, teaching you all things necessary for you to understand.

Brigham Young 8:176-177

On the contrary, there are certain truths brought to my mind by the aid of the Spirit of the Lord, that I have never forgotten. Truths deposited by the Holy Ghost are treasured up in the mind, and do not leave it.

Jedediah M. Grant 3:7

What shall be the result of the reception of the spirit? Christ told his disciples that it should bring all things whatsoever he had said to them to their remembrance. And was it to bring to memory only the things which had been heard? Or was it to reach back into the vista of the past and unfold to us some knowledge of our pre-existent state? Why not, since the spirit comprehends from the beginning to the end?

Aurelius Miner 20:233

We believe we are entitled to the gift of the Holy Ghost in extent according to the discretion and wisdom of God and our faithfulness; which gift brings all things to our remembrance, past, present, and to come, that are necessary for us to know, and as far as our minds are prepared to receive the knowledge of God revealed by that all-wise Agent.

Brigham Young 9:254

Jesus told them they should have the Holy Ghost, the Comforter; the Spirit should bring things past to their remembrance, it should enable them to comprehend something about the world and why it was organized and by whom; why man was placed upon it; what the position of the human family is in relation to the present, past and future; find out what God's dealings had been with the human family in ages gone and past, and His designs in relation to the world.

John Taylor 13:228

What else shall it do? It shall bring things past to your remembrance, so that you will be able to comprehend the things of God as they have existed in the different ages on the earth and with the Gods in the worlds, and you shall see eye to eye.

John Taylor 23:374
See also 13:266; 23:197

Shows You Things to Come

Then it [the Holy Ghost] should unfold things to come, it should draw back the curtain of futurity and by the inspiration and intelligence of that Spirit which proceeds from God, it should grasp the future. It should comprehend the destiny of the human family, and by the revelations which God should communicate, make known the life to come in the eternal worlds.

This is the kind of thing that the everlasting Gospel communicates, and it is the revelation of God to man. But the world, as I said before, know not the things of God, and they cannot comprehend them.

John Taylor 13:228

What else shall it do? It shall show you of things to come. You shall be enabled to look through the dark vista of the unborn future, to draw aside the veil of the invisible world, and comprehend the things of God; to know your destiny and the destiny of the human family, and the events that will transpire in coming ages and times. That is what the Holy Ghost will do, and therein is the difference between that Spirit and the little portion of that spirit which is given to every man to profit withal.

John Taylor 23:374

Leads You to Truth

What will it do for you? It will lead you into all truth, so that you will see eye to eye and comprehend the purposes of God; you will march in line; you will be under one instructor; you will have one Lord, one faith, one baptism; one God who is in all and through all, will inspire and guide and dictate you; you will not be split up and divided as the sectarians are — every man taking his own course, every man for himself and the devil for the whole; it will not be setting up human intellect above the intelligence and inspiration of the Almighty. Instead of this, all will bow to the dictates of Jehovah.

John Taylor 13:227

The Savior who undoubtedly knew best about the nature and character of this gift, said it should lead all who received it into all truth and show them things to come.

It should be more than that spirit which proceeds from God, filling the immensity of space and enlightening every man that comes into the world, the gift of the Holy Ghost should lead into all truth, and show them things to come. Furthermore, in speaking of its effects, the apostle says: "The spirit is given to every man to profit withal. To one is given faith."

Lorenzo Snow 14:303

Now what did Jesus tell His disciples the Holy Ghost should do when it came? He promised — "It shall lead you into all truth." What shall it do? Lead you into all truth — not into a diversity of sentiments, not into differences of doctrine, not into a variety of ordinances, but you shall see alike, comprehend alike and understand alike. "It shall lead you into all truth."

John Taylor 23:374
See also 3:61, 173-174; 20:233

Helps You to Be Steadfast to Truth

Brother Lyman has well said that it is this Spirit shed abroad upon the Latter-day Saints, bearing witness unto them of the truth — which is the witness of the Holy Ghost of the Father and of the Son — that makes them steadfast and immovable.

They cannot be turned away so long as they enjoy this Spirit; they cannot be turned away from the light of the Gospel and the liberties they enjoy in Christ Jesus; they cannot be converted to Catholicism, nor Methodism, nor any other ism; but if they fall into sin, if they violate their holy covenants, if they grieve the Holy Spirit from them, then they are left in great darkness.

Erastus Snow 25:71
See also 18:84

Bears Testimony to You

But in the ministry, where I labored earnestly, I began to comprehend more fully, through the inspiration of the Holy Spirit, what I had read and been taught, and so they became in my mind established facts, of which I was as absolutely certain as I was of my own existence; and from the beginning of my experience as an Elder in the Church until the present, if there has been a moment in my life when I have doubted the divinity and truthfulness of these things, it has escaped my notice, and it is today as much a matter of fact with me, as it is that I live.

> Joseph F. Smith 19:21

It is given to us to know these things for ourselves. God has said he will show these things unto us; and for this purpose the Holy Ghost has been imparted to all who are entitled to it through submission, which bears record of the Father and the Son, and also takes of the things of God and shows them unto man.

Convictions that we may previously have had respecting the truth the Holy Ghost confirms, giving us a positive assurance of their correctness, and through it we obtain a personal knowledge, not as one that has been told, but as one that has seen, felt, heard, and that knows for himself.

> Joseph F. Smith 19:263

Is there a conviction upon the minds of the people, when they have heard the Gospel preached, and where they have heard of it? Is there a conviction conveyed by the Holy Spirit that this is the Gospel of salvation? There is; and it cannot be denied without falsifying the truth.

> Brigham Young 8:131

It is for all, yea, every son and daughter of Adam to learn the will of God, to receive the testimony of the Spirit for him and herself, and not to depend alone upon the testimonies of these good men that God has raised up to fill the positions they occupy.

And if we should pin our faith to them, although we might realize consolation and even joy and satisfaction in hearing their testimonies, yet, unless we receive the inspiration of the Holy Spirit, the time will undoubtedly come when the winds will blow and the storms beat upon the house we thus may build and it will fall. What a deplorable condition we would then find ourselves in.

Is it not necessary for all to be capable of judging as to whether the testimonies of these men are of God or man? How can we know that what they testify of, is true? How can we know that they bear witness of the Almighty, or that they possess the holy Priesthood authorizing them to minister in the ordinances of the Gospel? I answer, only by and through the inspiration of that Holy Spirit which is given to all who diligently seek and obtain it according to the promise.

Then if we would know the Lord Jesus Christ, and his servants, who are in our midst, and that their testimonies are true, we must enjoy the light of the Spirit of the living God individually.

Joseph F. Smith 19:23

The Holy Ghost bears testimony to the man who receives it, and not to somebody else; and if he is pure enough to receive this gift, he has power enough in his heart to regulate his actions according to the law of God, instead of building golden calves.

Orson Pratt 7:180

The office of the Holy Spirit is to enlighten the minds of the people with regard to the things of God, to convince them at the time of their conversion of their having done the will of the Father, and to be in them an abiding testimony as a companion through life, acting as the sure and safe guide into all truth and filling them day by day with joy and gladness, with a disposition to do good to all men, to suffer wrong rather than to do wrong, to be kind and merciful, long suffering and charitable.

Joseph F. Smith 18:275

. . . When a man receives the Holy Ghost he has a testimony that can not deceive him or anybody else. . . .

But get the Holy Ghost and you have a testimony that cannot deceive you. It never deceived any man, and it never will. It is by this power and principle that the Elders of Israel have been sustained from the first day they commenced their labors until today.

Wilford Woodruff 16:38

A self-inspiring principle was upon them [those who received the Holy Ghost], which was tangible, giving them a knowledge of the cause they had espoused. They knew by revelation from God that the cause they had obeyed was true, it was revealed to them in a manner they could not dispute, and they knew for themselves. They were then established, as we heard this morning, upon the rock of revelation.

Lorenzo Snow 14:304
See also 18:276; 19:21

Reaffirms Your Testimony

Further, this unmistakable assurance, which is derived through yielding obedience to and practicing the principles of eternal life, is continually being confirmed, as it were, by "line upon line and precept upon precept," through the revelations of the Holy Spirit, which is a continuous and unfailing source of intelligence, of joy and happiness, drawing him who possesses it nearer unto God, and will eventually cause him to appear like unto his Maker.

Joseph F. Smith 18:276

Enables You to Teach Others and Testify to Them

If any man desires to act in the holy ministry he must first be baptized for a remission of his sins and receive the gift of the Holy Ghost, otherwise he cannot be a teacher unto others.

Charles W. Penrose 21:88

No man has authority to preach the Gospel and administer its ordinances without a commission from Jesus Christ; and the seal of such commission has always been, and always will be the gifts, blessings and endorsement of the Holy Ghost, which, not only leads to the form, but also to the power of godliness.

It is this that cheers the hearts of the Latter-day Saints, brings knowledge of things past, present and to come, unites and makes them in their testimony, hopes and aspirations, distinct from all the world — a peculiar people. . . . Bearing a faithful testimony, they [the missionaries] speak of that which they know and testify of that which they have experienced, saying "do the will of the Father and you shall know whether the doctrine is true or false". . . .

Where, outside of the Church of Jesus Christ of Latter-day Saints, is there a man authorized to make the promise of the knowledge of God by revelation as the reward of obedience to the principles of the Gospel? Who, beside the Elders of this Church are commissioned to perform ordinances in the name of the Father, Son and Holy Ghost through which, and by which the Comforter comes to the obedient penitent, leading him into all truth and showing him things to come? Who, beside them, are authorized by God, commissioned by Jesus and endorsed by the Holy Spirit to preach repentance, baptism and the laying on of hands?

Moses Thatcher 23:197

This Spirit animates our young brethren when faithfully attending to their duties while on missions, and it is this which enables them to say that the time so spent has been the happiest of their lives.

This enables our Elders, many of whom are to a great degree destitute of education, to stand before the learned, wise and noble, and the divines of the day, and declare the principles of the Gospel of Jesus. Who could do this under such circumstances without the Spirit of the Lord? I do not know the individual; and if there be those who could they are such as I referred to at the commencement of my remarks who, destitute of a knowledge of their own weakness, can stand up anywhere and speak with boldness, and exhibit themselves, whether it it wisdom or folly to do so.

None but those who enjoy the Spirit of the Lord, who are filled with the Holy Ghost, can stand before emperors, kings and wise men of the earth and speak the words of truth with all the simplicity and pleasure that children converse together [with].

Brigham Young 13:211

Enables You to Prophesy

What else can it [the Holy Ghost] do? It shall show you things to come; and if you were peradventure to declare any of these things you would become a prophet. This would be a terrible thing, to become a prophet! But Moses said when Joshua wanted him to rebuke certain ones and forbid them from prophesying in the camp of Israel, after asking him if he was jealous for his sake, "I would that all the Lord's people were prophets," because it would imply that they had obeyed this form of doctrine, that they were living in constant communion with the Holy Ghost.

Aurelius Miner 20:234

The Lord will reveal unto his servants the Prophets many things that are to come, and yet leave those who are not enlightened by the Spirit of Prophecy to wait until those things transpire before they are apprised of them. . . .

And to be a Prophet is to have the Spirit of Prophecy, and to have the testimony of Jesus, "for the testimony of Jesus is the Spirit of Prophecy," nothing more nor nothing less. The man who can testify that Jesus is the Christ has this testimony, and as he improves upon his gift he becomes a Prophet.

It is not one individual, it is not three, it is not twelve individuals, but it is for all the Saints who have the testimony of Jesus and live in the exercise of that testimony. A man that does not foresee by the Spirit of God, who does not learn things to come by it, is not living up to his privilege and profession, is not living in the enjoyment of that testimony which he has received; he is blinded by the mists of darkness and is liable to fall into a snare.

George A. Smith 10:67
See also 5:243

Helps You to See Yourself as God Sees You

The light of the Holy Ghost makes manifest men's deeds, and the Spirit of God is like a "two-edged sword, dividing the joints and the marrow," breaking, severing, cutting, piercing, penetrating, developing, and unfolding principles that we are almost entirely ignorant of, until they come to be developed.

When you have seen your ignorance and folly, you are inclined to say, "I thought I was a smart, good, able, intelligent man; but I have found out that I am a fool, and that I can do nothing to establish righteousness upon the earth, except the Lord God helps me to do it." When the Spirit of the living God was poured out more copiously upon you, it developed principles that were before latent within you. That Spirit enables you to see yourselves as the Lord sees you.

John Taylor 6:166

You have seen its effects upon us. It shall bring things past to your remembrance; it shall show you things to come; it shall make prophets of you; your sons and daughters shall see visions; the heavens shall be opened unto you; you shall know of your origin, comprehend who you are, what you are, where you are going to, the relationship which exists between you and your God; and there shall be a channel opened between the eternal worlds and you; and the purposes of God shall be made known unto you.

John Taylor 5:243

If we live continually so as to enjoy the guidance of the Holy Spirit of God, it will hold the mirror before our eyes, and enable us to understand our positions before God as plainly as we behold our natural faces in the glass; and if we have been heedless or negligent in the performance of our duties, it will be presented to our minds, and we will learn our faults, and if we sincerely repent, the whisperings of the Holy Spirit will prompt us as to the course we should take to make things right.

Erastus Snow 13:8

But if light breaks forth from any source and reflects upon the people, they then see the motes, the beams, and the dross in themselves. While the light maketh manifest, the Spirit of God reveals the secrets of the heart, and makes manifest those dark spots that exist among the Saints of God.

Jedediah M. Grant 4:123
See also 1:241

Guides You

For, unless the Spirit of the Lord directs and guides us, we are all of us in a very poor position indeed. In fact, it is very difficult for any of us to understand really and positively what would be for our best good without its aid.

John Taylor 6:105

Our business is then to find out what the Lord's will is, to guide us in our everyday life, not only to make us feel good, to exalt our spiritual nature, our emotions, our sentiments, our thoughts, not only that, but to guide us in our daily lives, so that all our acts may be squared according to the rule of right, that we may do that which is pleasing to our Heavenly Father, that we may learn to live so as not merely to do our own will, but to do the will of Him that has sent us here on the earth, and who has enlightened our minds in regard to the truth.

Charles W. Penrose 25:46

There is a consolation in our religion which goes to every heart, and by it every man, woman, and child may receive joy and satisfaction, while acting under the sweet influences of the Holy Spirit, having it within us to dictate and guide us in the path of virtue and truth.

Daniel H. Wells 9:94

And while we remain in the flesh He will not be a stranger to us; we will not walk in the dark like the majority of mankind, but we will be the children of the light, comprehending the truth as it is in Him, and seeing the path in which we should walk.

Charles W. Penrose 23:350

Men do not look at things as God looks at them, therefore it is indispensably necessary for each individual Latter-day Saint to have the Spirit of God within him, that he may do His will and not carry out his own views. . . .

I know it is true that God's ways are not as men's ways; and for a man to undertake to be a Latter-day Saint while groping in the dark by trusting wholly to the intelligence of his own mind, is the hardest work imaginable; it is the most laborious task that can be, for any individual on the earth to try to be what he ought to be before his God without the Holy Spirit to assist and guide him.

Brigham Young, Jr. 15:140
See also 5:124-125, and "Guide Us in Our Lives" in chapter 9.

Gives Premonitions/Warnings to You

I proclaim it as a truth, that when a man or woman enters into this Church and is baptized, repents of his or her sins, humbles himself and herself in the depth of humility before the Lord, determined with His help to forsake their sins, to put them away from them, I say, when a man or a woman comes to the Lord in that spirit and lives so that the Holy Ghost will rest upon them, that there will be no event of any importance from that time forward but what they will have some intimation respecting it, some premonition, and they will walk in the light, some to a greater extent than others, because some are more gifted than others, some live in such a manner as to have this developed within them to a greater extent.

But if they continue to cultivate this spirit, to live in the light of it, it will become a principle of unfailing revelation to them.

George Q. Cannon 22:104-105

Reflect upon past experience and upon the workings of the Spirit of God, and you will discover that you have often been forewarned of events long before they took place; and if you cast your minds into the book of the Spirit of God, and behold the acts and doings of the Lord in ages to come, you will find that the same principle that exists in the bosoms of the Gods is with you, though in a very undeveloped condition. Let your minds be set upon the will of God and upon His kingdom, and what will be withheld from your sight?

Orson Pratt 3:352

Increases Your Discernment

All who possess this inestimable gift [the Holy Ghost], this pearl of great price, have a continual thirst after righteousness. Without the aid of the Holy Spirit no mortal can walk in the straight and narrow way, being unable to discern right from wrong, the genuine from the counterfeit, so nearly alike can they be made to appear.

Joseph F. Smith 18:275

I will tell you a rule by which you may know the Spirit of God from the spirit of evil. The Spirit of God always produces joy and satisfaction of mind. When you have that Spirit you are happy; when you have another spirit you are not happy. The spirit of doubt is the spirit of the evil one; it produces uneasiness and other feelings that interfere with happiness and peace.

George Q. Cannon 15:375

I have proven to my satisfaction, according to the best knowledge I can gather, that man can be deceived by the sight of the natural eye, he can be deceived by the hearing of the ear, and by the touch of the hand; that he can be deceived in all of what are called the natural senses. But there is one thing in which he cannot be deceived.

What is that? It is the operations of the Holy Ghost, the Spirit and power of God upon the creature. It teaches him of heavenly things; it directs him in the way of life; it affords him the key by which he can test the devices of man, and which recommends the things of God. The sayings which I have quoted I have proven to be true, and I bear testimony to them.

Brigham Young 18:230

He therefore needs something to convince him, beyond all doubt, that the individuals prophesying were filled with the Holy Ghost, and that their predictions were true and could be depended upon; and then, whether they come to pass or not in his day, he knows they will be fulfilled in their times and in their seasons; and so with all other gifts.

He might see a miracle of any kind; he might see the laws of nature apparently overcome by a person calling himself a servant of God.

How does he know he is the servant of God, or that he performs that miracle by the power of God? Have not devils and fallen angels power? Did they not have mighty power in ancient days? Yes. Could they not smite the earth with plagues, and turn water into blood anciently, as Moses the servant of God did? Yes. Could not the wicked magicians of Egypt perform great signs by casting down their staves, and causing them to appear like serpents, performing great and marvellous things similar to those the Prophet Moses performed?

How is the natural man to judge? There is God on the one hand, and the Devil on the other; and if one is to judge naturally of these things, he would not be sure that the person performing a miracle before him was really inspired of God.

The gift and power of the Holy Ghost, as I have already observed, is the greatest evidence any man or woman can have concerning the kingdom of God. It is given expressly to impart to mankind a knowledge of the things of God. It is given to purify the heart of man, that he may by its power not only be able to understand its operations upon himself, but be able to understand its operations upon others also; and, indeed, if I could by any possible means independent of the Holy Ghost ascertain that a miracle was wrought of God, what particular benefit would it be to me?

Orson Pratt 7:179

Some may say, "Brethren, you who lead the Church, we have all confidence in you, we are not in the least afraid but what everything will go right under your superintendence; all the business matters will be transacted right; and if brother Brigham is satisfied with it, I am.''

I do not wish any Latter-day Saint in this world, nor in heaven, to be satisfied with anything I do, unless the Spirit of the Lord Jesus Christ, the spirit of revelation, makes them satisfied. I wish them to know for themselves and understand for themselves, for this would strengthen the faith that is within them.

Suppose that the people were heedless, that they manifested no concern with regard to the things of the kingdom of God, but threw the whole burden upon the leaders of the people, saying, "If the brethren who take charge of matters are satisfied, we are," this is not pleasing in the sight of the Lord.

Every man and woman in this kingdom ought to be satisfied with what we do, but they never should be satisfied without asking the Father, in the name of Jesus Christ, whether what we do is right. When you are inspired by the Holy Ghost you can understandingly say, that you are satisfied; and that is the only power that should cause you to exclaim that you are satisfied, for without that you do not know whether you should be satisfied or not.

You may say that you are satisfied and believe that all is right, and your confidence may be almost unbounded in the authorities of the Church of Jesus Christ, but if you asked God, in the name of Jesus, and received knowledge for yourself, through the Holy Spirit, would it not strengthen your faith? It would.

Brigham Young 3:44

I can say this for the Latter-day Saints, and I will say it to their praise and my satisfaction, if I were to preach false doctrine here, it would not be an hour after the people got out, before it would begin to fly from one to another, and they would remark, "I do not quite like that! It does not look exactly right! What did Brother Brigham mean? That did not sound quite right, it was not exactly the thing!"

All these observations would be made by the people, yes, even by the sisters. It would not sit well on the stomach, that is, on the spiritual stomach, if you think you have one. It would not sit well on the mind, for you are seeking after the things of God; you have started out for life and salvation, and with all their ignorance, wickedness and failings, the majority of this people are doing just as well as they know how.

And I will defy any man to preach false doctrine without being detected; and we need not go to the Elders of Israel, the children who have been born in these mountains possess enough of the Spirit to detect it. But be careful that you do not lose it! Live so that you will know the moment the Spirit of the Almighty is grieved within you. Do you ever see such times? I do. I watch you. . . .

You ought to live so that the very moment the Spirit of the Lord is grieved, stop that instantly, and turn the attention of every individual to something else that will retain the good Spirit of the Lord and give you an increase of it. This is the way to live.

Brigham Young 14:205

Then if we would know the Lord Jesus Christ, and his servants, who are in our midst, and that their testimonies are true, we must enjoy the light of the Spirit of the living God individually.

The possession of this heavenly knowledge is absolutely necessary to keep us in the paths of life and truth, for without it we cannot distinguish the voice of the true shepherd, which is spiritually discerned; and although we may be in fellowship with the Church, fully believing the counsels of our brethren to be dictated by wisdom, yet without something more than mere belief or supposition we cannot stand; and furthermore under such circumstances we cannot consistently claim that we have part or lot in the kingdom of God.

For as it is written, an actual knowledge to any person, that the course of life which he pursues is according to the will of God, is essentially necessary to enable him to have that confidence in God without which no person can obtain eternal life.

Joseph F. Smith 19:23

How does the child, or youth, immediately know when he performs the first wicked act of his life? Is there not within him a consciousness of right and wrong? This is a portion of divinity which lights every one who is born into the world, which acts as a monitor to the heart and soul, and never fails to impress the mind with an unmistakable sense of right and wrong.

This same spark of divinity, this monitor which speaks unmistakably to the understanding of the child, disapprovingly of his wrong, will speak, in just as unmistakable language, approvingly of good and righteous deeds.

Therefore I know what I declare to be true, because my conscience approves of my obeying the requirements of the Gospel; this inward monitor testifies to my spirit that in rendering this obedience I do right, and gives me the self-same assurance when I am in the discharge of any other duties, whether officiating in the capacity of an Elder or in the performance of those duties which, as an individual, I owe to society.

Joseph F. Smith 18:276
See also 4:191; 9:57; 10:145, 289; 19:341

Removes Veil of Darkness, Doubt and Fear

The Lord looks down upon our work and considers our ignorance, and so do those holy beings who surround his throne; but yet we know enough to do our duty, magnify our calling, and fulfill the object of our creation. And any man or community who have the Gospel of Christ, the holy Priesthood, and the power of the Holy Ghost that we have, possess a great advantage over the world; for they do not comprehend — they do not see nor understand the things that await them; they do not understand the dealings of God with them in any respect.

It is not so with the Latter-day Saints; for as long as they continue to receive the truth, their minds are opened to understand the character of the day and age in which we live, and all those trying scenes that are approaching us; the veil is taken from off the face of the earth, and we see things, to some extent, as they are.

We have received the gift of the Holy Ghost by the laying on of hands, and the veil of darkness, of doubt, and fear is taken from our minds, and we can see clearly where to go and what to do; and we feel that our spirit is right — that we are acceptable before the Lord our God, and are the subjects of his blessings.

Wilford Woodruff 8:268

Helps You Overcome Evil

The Prophet and Apostles had taught us the things of the kingdom so fully that we could not seek for more revelation; but we have been reviewing ourselves and our conduct to discover wherein we have not lived up to what has been revealed; and so great have been the apparent deficiencies, that the people have nearly all realized, when they examined themselves, that there was a great cause for lack of confidence in themselves and in each other.

This has been a general feeling; and it becomes us to bestir ourselves and obtain strength by the power of the Holy Ghost, so that we may overcome every evil propensity, resist the adversary of our souls in whatever shape he may present himself, and live our religion.

Franklin D. Richards 5:45

But all people born into the world receive a portion of divine light, and if they would grow up under the influence of that light and be actuated and guided by its whisperings all through their earthly career, it would lead them gradually up to the fountain of light, to "the Father of lights, with whom is no variableness, neither shadow of turning."

It would lead gradually to God, so that they could commune with God while they remain in the flesh; they would grow up nearer and nearer to Him, for they would choose the good and refuse the evil; they would take into their nature that which would lead them towards God, and they would repel from them that which would lead downward, they would discern the strait and narrow path that leadeth unto life, and they would avoid the broad road which leadeth unto destruction, in which so many of the human family have walked from the beginning.

It is because the people that dwell on the earth do not listen to the "still small voice" of that natural light which is born with them into the world, that they do not receive the things of God.
Charles W. Penrose 22:85

If we live according to our covenants we will always enjoy the light of truth, and if we live faithful enough we shall enjoy the blessing of the Holy Ghost to be our constant companion. In such case no person would turn either to the right hand or the left, in consequence of the motives, the sayings, or the doings of this one or that one; but they would march straightforward in the path that leads to eternal life; and if others stepped out of the way, they would walk straight along.

Without the power of the Holy Ghost a person is liable to go to the right or the left from the straight path of duty; they are liable to do things they are sorry for; they are liable to make mistakes; and when they try to do their best, behold they do that which they dislike.
Brigham Young 10:289
See also 16:27; 18:84; 24:290

Will Give Authority and Power

The Elders who have faithfully fulfilled their missions, warning all men who came within the sound of their voices, have identified themselves with the Savior, and with the Father, and with the Holy Ghost; and the Holy Ghost will abide with all such if they continue faithful; and herein consists the authority and power of every faithful servant of God in this and in all ages of the world.
Heber C. Kimball 11:145

The promise is to those who will repent and be baptized for the remission of sins; they shall receive "the gift of the Holy Ghost." What is it? It is a greater and higher endowment of the same spirit which enlightens every man that comes into the world; a greater power given unto us as an abiding witness, to be a light to our feet and a lamp to our path; as a restraint against sin, to guide us into all truth, to open up the vision of the mind, to bring things past to our remembrance, and to make manifest things to come.
Charles W. Penrose 23:350

Helps You Understand Your Priesthood Duties

I would say to bishops, and to all men in authority, we should have an interest in carrying on this work. We should labor to get the Spirit of God. It is our right, our privilege, and our duty to call upon the Lord, that the vision of our mind may be opened, so that we may see and understand the day and age in which we are living. It is your privilege, and mine too, to know the mind and will of the Lord concerning our duties, and if we fail to seek after this, we neglect to magnify our calling.

Wilford Woodruff 21:283

It is the right and privilege of every Elder in Israel to enjoy the Holy Ghost, and the light of it, to know everything which concerns himself and his individual duties, but it is not his right and privilege to dictate his superior in office, nor to give him counsel, unless he is called upon to do so, then he may make suggestions; and if the people of a ward are living in the faithful performance of their several duties, their faith and their prayers will be concentrated before the Lord, in the name of Jesus, for and in behalf of their Bishop, that he may know his business and be made fully capable to fulfill the duties of his calling to the honor of God and the salvation of the people.

Brigham Young 11:135

The man who has the priesthood, who is filled with the Holy Ghost, is to be guided and dictated by it in the way of happiness and life. It is very necessary for us to have these things laid before us frequently, that we may be put in remembrance of our duties.

The organized spirit which God gave us is the one which conceives through the revelations that are given from on high. The nature and the character of those teachings that come from the Priesthood are such that we comprehend them: the Spirit manifests them unto us as they are. By it we learn our duties to God and man. We are taught by it to shun the evil and cleave unto that which is good. We understand this, if we are in the path of duty.

Lorenzo Snow 9:21

For every man called to occupy any position can, if he seeks aright, obtain the spirit of that calling, and in that there is peace and joy and satisfaction, so that he is paid in his labors in any office which he may be called to fill. . . .

We can get a measure of the spirit of this calling today, and by the power thereof we can have communion with our Father. Not only through the living oracles in a Church capacity, but as individual members of the Church we can come near unto the Lord, so that there will be no barrier between us and him, and so that his Spirit can come upon us freely, and the light of God can illuminate our souls and so direct us that we may have the life and the strength of this eternal priesthood.

For this priesthood is a reality and not a mere name; it is not a mere calling in word, but an office which confers upon us power and influence that comes from the Almighty. I know that men holding the priesthood, and who magnify it and receive the spirit and power of it, are different from other men, their influence and motives are different, their feelings are different and the spirit and influence they carry with them are different.

Charles W. Penrose 21:48, 49

Will Teach You and Your Family Your Duties

When I speak of our duty it applies to all, male and female. It is the right of the mother who labors in the kitchen, with her little prattling children around, to enjoy the Spirit of Christ, and to know her duty with regard to those children; but it is not her duty and privilege to dictate to her husband in his duties and business. If that mother or wife enjoys the gift and power of the Holy Ghost, she will never intrude upon the rights of her husband.

It is the right and privilege of the husband to know his duty with regard to his wives and children, his flocks and his herds, his fields and his possessions; though I have seen women who, I thought, actually knew more about the business of life than their husbands themselves did, and were really more capable of directing a farm, the building of a house, and the management of flocks and herds, etc., than the men were; but if men were to live up to their privileges this would not be the case; for it is their right to claim the light of truth and that intelligence and knowledge necessary to enable them to carry on every branch of their business successfully.

Brigham Young 11:135
See also 13:272-273, and "Raise Our Children Properly" in chapter 9.

Builds Self-Confidence

There is a monitor in the heart of every individual, and a man or woman, who will obey its dictations, and whose intentions are to do right all the day long, need not be afraid of anything, for they will have confidence; they shall have confidence before God; they shall have confidence before the Saints, and be enabled to claim the promises, and there is no power that can hinder; there is no power that can stand against them, but they shall prevail.

Ezra T. Benson 3:78

Persons must so live that they can enjoy the light of the Holy Spirit, or they will have no confidence in themselves, in their religion, or in their God, and will sooner or later turn from the faith. They are in sorrow, and leave in search of something that will satisfy their minds.

Brigham Young 8:65

They comprehend themselves and the great object of their existence. They also comprehend the designs of the wicked one, and the designs of those who serve him; they comprehend the designs of the Almighty in forming the earth, and mankind upon it, and the ultimate purpose of all His creations. It [the Holy Ghost] leads them to drink at the fountain of eternal wisdom, justice, and truth; they grow in grace, and in the knowledge of the truth as it is in Jesus Christ, until they see as they are seen, and know as they are known.

Brigham Young 1:241

Strengthens Your Body

Latter-day Saints, are not these things worthy of living for? Suppose that you could have the privilege, by living only one week in strict obedience to all the laws of the kingdom, to have these blessings.

I verily believe that there are not many Latter-day Saints, but who, if they knew that they could enjoy all the blessings of the ancients and have the visions of the heavens laid open to their minds, so that they could have before them the past, the present, and the future, so that they could understand the things of God, would live very faithful, and be of one heart and of one mind.

Would not every one who heard such promises try to obtain the prize, to enjoy the blessings promised? The counsels and instructions of those whom God has appointed would be fresh before them every moment; when they arose in the morning it would be the first thing they would think of, and it would be the last thing at night. They would be able to do twice as much labor as when their minds are not upon the things of God.

Their minds would be so entirely swallowed up that they would feel like Alma and others, while among the priests of king Noah, when they had burdens upon their backs; their burdens were made light so that they were able to bear them cheerfully, and so it would be with the Latter-day Saints.

Let them have that Spirit one week, and they would find their bodies stronger and more active, and they would almost forget whether they had been to their breakfast, dinner, or supper, their minds would be so completely swallowed up with heavenly things, and everything would prosper.

You are to claim blessings by your conduct, you are so instructed; some are apt to be so neglectful and remiss in their duties that they are not able to claim them. They forget what is in store for them, and do not pray for the Spirit to impress those blessings upon their minds, but suffer their minds to be drawn out too much upon temporal business instead of the things of God, and become weary in mind and body, so that they feel like neglecting the more prominent duties, such as family prayer and many others.

This is because they do not enjoy sufficient of the Spirit of the Lord, for it is able to strengthen every one of you. Look at the promises made to the missionaries, "He that shall go forth to preach the Gospel without purse or scrip shall not be weary, nor darkened in spirit nor in body."

What is it that strengthens them so that they do not become weary in body and mind? The Elders abroad are called upon to labor diligently, and many times to sit up almost all night to teach the pure principles of eternal life, and when they lie down they rest perfectly calm as though they were not weary, and arise invigorated with faith, intelligence, and power; their minds and bodies are strengthened by the power of God.

Orson Pratt 3:349-350

Pray without ceasing, and in everything give thanks. Is it not a hard task to live this religion without enjoying the spirit of it? Such a course worries the feelings, fills a person with sorrow and affliction, and makes him miserable. The easiest life to live, by any mortal being on the earth, is to live in the light of God's countenance, and have fellowship with his Son Jesus Christ. I know this by my own experience. In this course there is no darkness, no sorrow, no grief. The power of the Spirit of God has preserved me in the vigour of youth, and I am as active as a boy.

How is it with you who do not enjoy the spirit of your religion? It is a hard life for you to live; and you had better, from this day, take a course to enjoy the Spirit of the Lord; then you will be numbered with the wise.

Brigham Young 8:198

Live so that you will know the moment the Spirit of the Almighty is grieved within you. Do you ever see such times? I do. I watch you. I see, for instance, a company of young people go and mingle, perhaps, with old people, and hear them laughing, joking, and talking nonsense and folly.

By and by darkness comes — leanness of the soul; and one says, "My head don't feel right; my heart is not right; my nerves are not right; I do not know what is the matter, but I do not enjoy myself here this evening."

Do you know what is the matter? You ought to live so that the very moment the Spirit of the Lord is grieved, stop that instantly, and turn the attention of every individual to something else that will retain the good Spirit of the Lord and give you an increase of it. This is the way to live.

Brigham Young 14:205

Brings Happiness to You

It has always been a great satisfaction to my mind, and a source of pleasure, to speak of the things of the kingdom of God, especially on those occasions on which the Lord has condescended to bless me with a portion of his Spirit; for the Spirit of the Lord gives joy and satisfaction to all those who are made partakers of it, whether it be the speaker or the hearer; and without that Spirit no person can expect to enjoy any great degree of happiness in this life or in that which is to come.

It is contrary to the nature of happiness for us to undertake to enjoy ourselves independent of the approbation of Heaven, and independent of the Holy Spirit which the Almighty pours out upon those who are honest and upright before him. There is no happiness in anything else; there is no place worthy of being called a place of happiness only in the enjoyment of the favour of God and of his Holy Spirit. And those persons are truly blessed who have the greatest share of that Spirit abiding with them; and when that Spirit withdraws from the hearts of mankind, they are truly cursed.

In the Spirit of the Lord there is peace, there is joy, there is light, there is truth, there is hope, and there is faith. Without that Spirit all is darkness, all is wretchedness, and all is shut up and closed as it were to the human mind, and future hope, or hope of future blessings and exaltation, is cut off.

Orson Pratt 8:306

All people desire to be happy. You cannot find an individual that does not wish comfort and ease. You can obtain happiness in no other way than by unreservedly submitting yourselves to your God. Let him lead us through paths of affliction and cause suffering and trouble to come upon us, still there is that consolation and comfort within that the world cannot give nor take away. That is the only solid comfort there is in this life.

Men cannot enjoy comfort and satisfaction in the accumulation of wealth. Wealth never was the source of happiness to any person. It cannot be; it is not in the nature of things; for contentment exists only in the mind. In the mind there is happiness — in the mind there is glory.

Place a man in extreme poverty, and let him possess the sweet, benign influences of the Spirit of the Lord, and you will find a happy man and a cheerful countenance; while the man who does not possess the Spirit of heaven, though he may possess all this world can afford beside, is almost constantly in sorrow and trouble.

Brigham Young 7:159

There are many things pertaining to our everyday duties, which if we clearly understood by the light of the Spirit, we would escape many things which cause unhappiness. It is the want of clearly understanding the will of the Lord under all circumstances that causes us to fall into many of the evils that we pass through in life.

Orson Pratt 15:230

Without the light of the Spirit of Christ, no person can truly enjoy life.

Brigham Young 3:66

You cannot have it [heaven here] unless you enjoy the Spirit of the Lord, not one of you; you cannot find comfort, solace, or bliss without the Spirit of the Lord. . . .

Only let us have the Spirit of the Lord and we can be happy; while the things of this world, that are so eagerly sought after, all point directly to the grave. Men and women who are trying to make themselves happy in the possession of wealth or power will miss it, for nothing short of the gospel of the Son of God can make the inhabitants of the earth happy, and prepare them to enjoy heaven here and hereafter.

Brigham Young 11:329

Do you not think it will pay a man or a woman to keep the commandments of God? It will, and when we enjoy the Holy Spirit, when we are trying to live our religion here on the earth, we are the happiest people on God's footstool, no matter what our circumstances may be.

I do not care whether we are rich or poor, whether in happiness or affliction, if a man is living his religion and enjoys the favor and Spirit of God, it makes no difference to him what takes place on the earth. There may be earthquakes, war, fire or sword in the land, but he feels that it is all right with him. That is the way I feel today.

Wilford Woodruff 18:35

I will tell you a rule by which you may know the Spirit of God from the spirit of evil. The Spirit of God always produces joy and satisfaction of mind. When you have that Spirit you are happy; when you have another spirit you are not happy. The spirit of doubt is the spirit of the evil one; it produces uneasiness and other feelings that interfere with happiness and peace.

George Q. Cannon 15:375

The man who has the priesthood, who is filled with the Holy Ghost, is to be guided and dictated by it in the way of happiness and life. It is very necessary for us to have these things laid before us frequently, that we may be put in remembrance of our duties.

Lorenzo Snow 9:21

This Spirit animates our young brethren when faithfully attending to their duties while on missions, and it is this which enables them to say that the time so spent has been the happiest of their lives.

Brigham Young 13:210
See also 6:164

Brings Prosperity

We have no need of being roused from a state of lethargy, if we will let the Spirit lead us; and the Lord will prosper us; for the man and the woman that keeps His Spirit is right: with it the people can bring as much again to pass as they can otherwise. They are stronger in their minds and in their judgments, and are more capable of gathering around them the comforts of life for their subsistence.

Instead of "Mormonism" disqualifying us, it qualifies us for all things that ought to be done. Let us be careful not to allow the enemy to come and sow tares, but keep alive to the duties enjoined upon us.

Daniel H. Wells 5:42

I can see, also, many times when the Spirit of the Lord whispered to me, and I scarcely knew whether it was my own thoughts and imaginations or whether it was the revelations of the Spirit; yet it seemed to be the Spirit of the Lord, and I followed the teachings, and was prospered in so doing.

Orson Pratt 15:230

Brethren, if you want to get rich, live so as to enjoy the Spirit of the Lord. You will then know exactly what to do in all matters. You want the spirit of wisdom in all your business transactions, and just as much in farming as anything else.

We want the Spirit of the Lord from the least chore of labor that we perform, to the highest spiritual duty devolving upon the highest man in the kingdom of God. We want the Spirit of the Lord to guide and direct us through this world, to teach us in spiritual things and in temporal things, that we may learn how to gain to ourselves the riches of eternity, and secure to ourselves eternal lives. God bless you. Amen.

Brigham Young 15:43

Will Do Many Things for You

The Spirit is to purify, sanctify, justify, to give love, joy, peace, long-suffering, patience, hope, and all these great and glorious effects that are promised in the word of God.

Orson Pratt 14:178

We feel that we are in possession of the principles of eternal life, which are as a well of water within us and around us, and of which we drink and participate in when we live our religion. It emanates from God, issues from the Fountain of life and truth — the Source of all intelligence, and is imparted to us through the medium of the everlasting Gospel. It has enlightened our minds, enlarged our understandings, extended our feelings, informed our judgment — has warmed up our affections to God and holiness; has nourished and cherished us, and put us in possession of principles that we know will abide forever and forever.

John Taylor 7:318

It will never hurt you, but will give life, joy, peace, satisfaction, and contentment; it is light, intelligence, strength, power, glory, wisdom, and finally, it comprehends the kingdoms that are, that were, or that will be, and all that we can contemplate or desire, and will lead us to everlasting life.

Brigham Young 11:329

Enables You to Know About the
Inhabitants of the World

If you could just humble yourselves until your eyes should be enlightened by the Spirit of God, by the spirit of intelligence, you may understand things the world cannot see; and understand that it is the

privilege of every person to know the exact situation of the inhabitants
of the earth, for themselves. The ancient Apostles saw it; Jesus Christ
knew all about it; and the Prophets before them prophesied, and wrote,
and preached about what was then upon the earth, what had been, and
what would be.

> Brigham Young 3:89

The Holy Ghost reveals unto you things past, present, and to
come; it makes your minds quick and vivid to understand the handy
work of the Lord. Your joy is made full in beholding the footsteps of
our Father going forth among the inhabitants of the earth; this is
invisible to the world, but it is made visible to the Saints, and they
behold the Lord in His providences, bringing forth the work of the last
days.

> Brigham Young 4:22

Builds Brotherly Consideration for Others

Our religion is not something in which we alone are personally
concerned, but the moment people are put in possession of the Spirit of
God they begin to feel interested about the welfare of others. . . .

Inspired by the Spirit of God they [the Elders] feel as God feels
towards the human family — a desire to bless, comfort, and instruct
and to lead them in the paths of life. God places this principle in the
hearts of his servants — it emanates from him and is part of his nature;
and inasmuch as the Elders are dictated by this spirit in their acts
insomuch do they resemble their heavenly Father, who is full of
benevolence and "causes his sun to rise on the evil and on the good,
and makes the rain to descend on the just and on the unjust;" and hence
whenever we become acquainted with the principles of life ourselves
we feel a desire to communicate the same unto others.

> John Taylor 15:284-285

It is the duty of every one to labor day by day to promote each
other's happiness, and also to study the well-being of mankind. When
we take a course opposite to this, we become uneasy, unhappy and
discontented; we are not satisfied with anything that is around us; our
food, our raiment, our habitations and all that we possess becomes an
annoyance to us; now what is the cause of this?

It certainly does not originate with the Spirit of God, for that will
never render anyone unhappy. You all understand, when you are in the
right, that it is the spirit of the world, or that spirit which controls the
world, which causes people to feel in this way; and unless they drive it
far from them it will lead them down to sorrow, misery and death. It is

a spirit that inclines to kill and destroy, and that inclines the wicked to waste away everything there is upon the earth.

Heber C. Kimball 10:240

Enables You to Recognize the Holy Ghost in Other People

Hence, for men spiritually unenlightened to be unable to comprehend the things of God is not peculiar to the dispensation in which we live, but it has been so in every age when God made known His will to the children of men. Such individuals may come in contact with the greatest of Heaven's children and may associate with them day by day, and yet through not having the Spirit they will fail to recognize their nobility of character, and that they are divinely inspired.

Some of the members, even, of Jesus' own family, as we learn from the sacred record, ridiculed him; they could not recognize that their own brother, the son of their mother, was the Son of God, who was to die for the sins of the world; although they had been brought up with Jesus from childhood. They failed to recognize it for the very reason that Joseph Smith, and Brigham Young, and every prophet and apostle that ever lived on the face of the earth have not been recognized by many of their associates.

If their minds had been enlightened by the Spirit of God they would have recognized the men of God, and could have comprehended the things of God and the plan of salvation; they could have seen God in it all; every feature would have beamed with the godhead and with the divinity; they would have recognized it as an emanation from heaven and would have sustained the Son of God as the being he professed to be, and which he was; and his Apostles would have had no occasion to have gone about as they did — persecuted and hated, and afterwards cruelly killed for the testimony of Jesus which they bore to mankind.

Noah would not have had such a difficult work in trying to convince the inhabitants of the earth in his day of the message God had given to him, neither would all the prophets from this day down have had the difficulty they had. No man with his natural wisdom can comprehend the things of God; man never did do it and never can do it.

George Q. Cannon 11:334

Builds Unity

"Well," says one, "If we are influenced by the same Spirit — if we all do as the Spirit dictates, shall we not be one?" If all the people

— the individuals that compose this community, were individually to
be operated upon by the Spirit of God — were all enlightened by that
Spirit that reveals the will of God, that makes known his purposes, and
that imparts to the benighted soul an understanding of the purposes of
the Almighty, so that we could appreciate them, there is no doubt in
my mind but that the people would all see alike, and consequently act
alike.

But is this the case? With all our advantages — with all the
instructions that have been given — with Heaven's kindness in the
continued, unremitting stream of revelation that has been poured out
upon us for a score of years and more, have we become so enlightened
— got understanding so that we all see alike, that we all understand
alike?

We have but to look and contemplate what we see exhibited around
us to become satisfied at once that this is not the case with us as a
people. If it were so, such admonitions as are called out from the
Presidency of the Church would be uncalled for; they would be
unnecessary; the people would not be admonished to be more united,
to be more diligent and strict in remembering the principles and in
practicing the instructions that are from time to time imparted unto
them.

Amasa M. Lyman 6:78, 79

In order for us to be prepared to do the will of God, and be in a
position to build up His kingdom upon the earth, and to carry out His
purposes, we must not only become united and act as the heart of one
man, but we must obtain the Holy Spirit of God, and the mind and will
of God concerning us, and be governed and controlled by it in all of
our movements and acts, in order to be safe, and to secure unto
ourselves salvation.

Wilford Woodruff 4:191

If men were in the possession of the gift of the Holy Ghost, it
would lead them into all truth, and there would be one Lord, as the
Scriptures say, and one faith and one baptism. Hence, one of the old
Prophets, clothed upon by the Spirit of the Living God, looked through
the vista of future ages and contemplated events that should transpire in
the latter-days, and said: "When the Lord shall bring again Zion, her
watchmen shall see eye to eye."

There will be no confusion there, no difference of sentiment there.
They will place themselves under the guidance of the Great Eloheim,
and under His inspiration they will be enabled to speak as they are

moved upon by the Holy Ghost; and the Spirit of God, as it did formerly, will take of the things of God and shew them unto them.

John Taylor 25:212-213
See also 4:191; 6:208; 11:135; 19:252; 22:366; (13:227; 23:374 are quoted in "Leads You to Truth" — this chapter)

Brings Peace

You want to live so that your minds will be filled with his Spirit; and to do this, you need not take a mission to the sun, to the moon, or to the stars, to find out their distances or how much they weigh. But are you acquainted with your homes? You answer, "Yes."

Well, then, do right at home, do not do wrong, do not quarrel at home, do not stir up disunion, do not, in a word, do anything to bring about a pandemonium instead of a paradise; but do that which brings peace — that which produces the spirit of peace and of heaven.

But where division of sentiment, diversity of feeling, and discord exist, the principles of heaven are not there; the principles of peace are not there. Study these principles, and for what purpose? Why, that it may stir up the spirit of peace within you — that the spirit of peace may be, not a casual visitor, but a constant attendant — that he may take up his abode with you.

And when an individual takes up his abode with you, then you do not consider him a transient visitor, but there is his home — there is where he lodges, where he stays, where he imparts blessings — if he is a minister of blessings, where he imparts good, if he has any good to impart.

Amasa M. Lyman 5:310

There is a consolation in our religion which goes to every heart, and by it every man, woman, and child may receive joy and satisfaction, while acting under the sweet influences of the Holy Spirit, having it within us to dictate and guide us in the path of virtue and truth.

When the Spirit of the Lord influences any man, especially the true and faithful Saint, it fills him with joy and peace, and makes him humble in the performance of duties.

The Spirit of the Lord carries with it its own reward. A person deprived of this influence meets with difficulties upon every hand. It is only by being obedient and submitting to the counsel of God in all things, that we can fully enjoy that good Spirit.

Daniel H. Wells 9:94
See also 3:343; 8:121; 11:333

Will Strengthen and Comfort You During Trials

And if you open a door that this Spirit will take up his abode with you, then that fountain which will be opened up will become very plenteous in its supplies; it will become so to you because you welcome the Holy Spirit there, and you study to cultivate within you such a feeling that the Spirit will love to tarry with you day by day; and its book of instructions will be opened to you, so that each succeeding day will give you an increase of knowledge, and you find yourselves able to comprehend one degree of light and knowledge after another, until your whole soul will be swallowed up in your love for the truth, your affections will be bound up in the truth; for which you will be willing to sacrifice all. . . .

What will this prepare you for? For any contingency that may arise; and you will be contented in the storm and confident of what the result will be.

If the storm-clouds lour around you, you will be comforted by the sunshine of the Spirit of God; and however dark the clouds that may lour around, you will find that Spirit to be your companion; you will see the sunshine that opens to you the prospect of happiness, of glory, and of eternal life when the clouds shall pass away.

Why will this be the case? Because you have prepared yourselves that the Spirit might be in you, having cultivated it all through your lives. Then you have a devotion to the truth, and the Spirit of truth will tarry with you, and by-and-by you will become fully devoted to the truth; your affections will become pure and holy; and then when you are purified and made holy, you will not depart from the truth, nor go into darkness and apostacy, because the sunlight of truth is within you.

Amasa M. Lyman 5:310

Nor will he, if we are faithful, permit the wicked to do anything that will not ultimately prove beneficial to those who love and obey Him. With the companionship of the Holy Spirit the doctrines of the Priesthood will distil upon our minds as the dews of heaven, and we have nothing to fear. The time may be near at hand when men's souls will be tried, but those possessing the inspiration of the Almighty, will bear the test as the faithful and true in other ages have done.

Moses Thatcher 23:212

The consolations of the Holy Spirit of our Gospel comfort the hearts of men and women, old and young, in every condition of this mortal life. The humble, the meek, and faithful are all the time consoled and comforted by the Spirit of the Gospel that we preach; consequently, their comfort, happiness, joy, and peace must be received from the fountainhead. As Jesus says, "In the world ye shall have tribulation, but in me ye have peace," so we say to ourselves, so we say to the Saints; in the Lord ye have joy and comfort, and the light of truth which shines upon your path.

Brigham Young 4:22

We convert people by preaching repentance, and baptizing them for the remission of sins, and laying on of hands for the gift of the Holy Ghost; which spirit broods over them continually for their good, heals their bodies, enlightens their minds, and makes them humble, meek, and harmless as little children.

Brigham Young 1:240, 241

Helps You to Obey Commandments

The Spirit may rest upon many and reveal to them the wonderful things of God; but when it does it will prompt them to obey the commands of the Lord Jesus. Is this the fact? It is.

Brigham Young 14:135

And it was hoped and expected that when the Holy Ghost descended upon men and women they would be filled with the spirit of obedience, and that their understandings would be so awakened that they would begin to comprehend the object God had in view in restoring the everlasting Gospel to the earth.

George Q. Cannon 11:33

If I could see every one of the Elders with their wives and children as obedient to every requirement made of them — the children to the parents, the wives to the husbands, and the husbands to the Priesthood — as the Twelve are — my soul would be happy. I will say further; those of the Twelve that travel the most and serve God, are the most obedient.

Some of the Elders get up and tell you that you must be obedient to the counsel that is given you, which is all right, but I wish the people could know my feelings in regard to this. I have never asked but one thing of the Latter-day Saints, and that is for them to serve the Lord our God with an undivided heart.

One says, "I knew brother Joseph, but I do not know much about brother Brigham." I do not care for this; the question with me is this, do you know Jesus and the Holy Spirit ? I do not care if you never hear any more about brother Brigham, so far as my personal feelings are concerned, if you will only live under the influence of that Spirit which comes from God. When the brethren are traveling and preaching they have the spirit of obedience; and while we are here preaching to you the Spirit of the Lord broods over the congregation, your countenances are lit up with heavenly intelligence, your hearts are one, and you are ready to observe every word of counsel that is given to you, and each and every one feels to say, "It is my delight to do the will of God.

When we were children in this Church — had just received the spirit of the holy Gospel — how did we feel? We felt and we were as submissive as little children, ready to do the will and bidding of the Elders, just as fast as we learned it. We were as obedient to those who were set to counsel us as the child is to its mother; we had no disposition to rebel, but our feeling was, "let me know the will of God, and I will do it."

> Brigham Young 10:310-311

Now we are livened up again, we feel the lively emotions of the Spirit of God, and we are ready to do anything that may be counselled by whoever has the right to counsel. We are ready to walk in the path of strict obedience. Let us keep right from this time forth, and not go to sleep again, nor let the enemy sow tares as he did before.

> Daniel H. Wells 5:42
> See also 16:38

Will Purify Your Heart

The gift and power of the Holy Ghost, as I have already observed, is the greatest evidence any man or woman can have concerning the kingdom of God. It is given expressly to impart to mankind a knowledge of the things of God. It is given to purify the heart of man, that he may by its power not only be able to understand its operations upon himself, but be able to understand its operations upon others also.

> Orson Pratt 7:179

Blesses You

God has made promises unto His people. If His people do their part He will fulfill those promises; He will give that portion of His Spirit that is necessary to impart unto them everything that their circumstances may require.

> George Q. Cannon 24:179

It is our privilege to follow the dictates of the Spirit of the Lord, and to have it for our guide and companion; and by doing this the blessings of the heavens will be upon us as fast as we are prepared to receive them.

> Wilford Woodruff 8:270

It [the Holy Ghost] is the system of government God has revealed to the children of men that gives people a right to the ordinances, blessings and privileges of the Gospel of Christ, and without that they have not any legal right to them, and cannot claim them.

Brigham Young 10:323

Gives Inclinations unto Righteousness

We are exhorted to make our own heaven, our own paradise, our own Zion. How is this to be done? By hearkening diligently to the voice of the Spirit of the Lord that entices to righteousness, applauds truth, and exults continually in goodness.

This Spirit is the companion of every faithful person! Listen to its whisperings, and pursue with alacrity the path it points out. In this way we may all grow in grace and in the knowledge of the truth, and by so doing we shall honour the life we now possess, while by pursuing an opposite course we disgrace it. This life is worth as much to us as any life in the eternities of the Gods.

Brigham Young 9:170

When the Spirit of the Lord rests upon a community, they naturally are inclined to feel after the Lord their God, and they are inclined unto righteousness, and they like the influence of that Spirit which leads into all truth; it is sweet and very delicious to them.

Jedediah M. Grant 4:123

Brings Desire to Pray Without Ceasing

I know that in the world we have tribulation, sorrow and mourning, but in Christ we have joy; and when we have the Spirit of Christ we feel to pray without ceasing, and in everything to give thanks to God our heavenly Father.

Brigham Young 10:314

Places You in Communion with God

Then it is that the Spirit takes of the things of God and shows them unto us; then it is that we are brought into communion with our heavenly Father; then it is that we have a hope that enters within the vail, whither Christ our forerunner is gone; then it is that we have an unction from the Holy One, as they had in former times, that will teach us the principles of light, and life, and intelligence, pertaining to our present and future existence.

Then it is that the darkness with which the world is beclouded is removed, and the light of heaven is permitted to permeate our minds and impart light and intelligence thereunto; then it is that we are sons of

God; and it does not yet appear what we shall be, says the sacred writer; "but when he who is our life shall appear, then shall we appear like unto him in glory;" it is through this principle, and this life, light and intelligence, and that through obedience to the commands of God.

John Taylor 18:199

I am grateful for another peaceful opportunity of partaking of the sacrament with the Saints; for as often as we do so worthily, we renew our covenants with our Heavenly Father, and receive the promise of the Holy Spirit through whom comes communion with God. To us such communion is worth more than all earthly things.

Moses Thatcher 26:204

The ordinance of baptism for the remission of sins being essential, so is the ordinance of the laying on of hands, that men may receive the Holy Spirit; or, in other words, the laying on of hands is the medium that God has instituted for His children to be placed in communication with Himself, that they may receive the Spirit that leads and guides and directs unto all truth, that brings things past to our remembrance, that shows us things to come, that opens up the visions of heaven and makes known unto us the mind and will of God.

John Morgan 25:77

We were also told that the Holy Ghost would place us in communication with God; that it would take of the things of God and show them unto us, and that we should know for a certainty, each of us for ourselves, of the truths that had been proclaimed unto us.

John Taylor 13:226
See also 23:350

Enables You to Be One with God

If the all-wise Spirit gains an existence in man, it endeavors to influence and persuade him to become one with God, as it is one with Him.

Orson Pratt 2:341

Helps You to Do God's Will

Men do not look at things as God looks at them, therefore it is indispensably necessary for each individual Latter-day Saint to have the Spirit of God within him, that he may do His will and not carry out his own views. . . .

I know it is true that God's ways are not as men's ways; and for a man to undertake to be a Latter-day Saint while groping in the dark by trusting wholly to the intelligence of his own mind, is the hardest work imaginable; it is the most laborious task that can be, for any individual on the earth to try to be what he ought to be before his God without the Holy Spirit to assist and guide him.

Brigham Young, Jr. 15:140

For as it is written, an actual knowledge to any person, that the course of life which he pursues is according to the will of God, is essentially necessary to enable him to have that confidence in God without which no person can obtain eternal life. . . . But when he has this knowledge, and most assuredly knows that he is doing the will of God, his confidence can be equally strong that he will be a partaker of the glory of God.

Joseph F. Smith 19:23
See also 25:46 (quoted in ''Guides You'' in this chapter)

Gives Visions of the Spirit World

We can have a glimpse occasionally, through the revelations of the Spirit to us, of the glory there is awaiting us, and sometimes when men and women are approaching death — when they are ready to step out of this existence into the other — the veil becomes so thin that they behold the glories of the eternal world, and when they come back again — as some have, we all probably have met those who have been snatched from death — they come back to this mortal existence with a feeling of regret.

They have had a foretaste of the glory that awaited them; they have had a glimpse of that glory that is behind the veil; and the love of life is so completely lost — the love of earthly home and friends is so completely taken from them, that they desire with all their hearts to take their exit from this life into that glorious life which they knew was on the other side of the veil.

George Q. Cannon 26:192-193

When we have the Holy Spirit, all is right, and we feel satisfied; the visions of the Almighty and of the heavens are before us night and day, and we have confidence in the holy Gospel, in the work of the Lord, in the Priesthood, and in those who hold that authority upon this earth.

Ezra T. Benson 3:63

Brings Recognition of God's Hand

Who does comprehend the work which the Lord is accomplishing with such rapidity? Why there is not a Latter-day Saint within the sound of my voice, no matter how young, humble, ignorant, or void of understanding he or she may be, who knows anything about the Spirit or the things of God, but can see divinity and the power of God manifested in every move made, and in all that has been done in connection with this work, from the beginning of their experience to the present time.

They see God and recognize His hand in this work; and they also understand that man could not bestow upon him the blessings of peace and joy that they have in the Holy Ghost.

George Q. Cannon 11:333

Prepares Us for Godhood

This great future reward is worth living for, and this is what we should seek for, even for the enlightenment of the Spirit. This is what we should endeavor to cultivate in all our business transactions, and in all our concerns here in life.

If we cultivate this Spirit, it will increase upon us, and it will grow brighter and brighter, until the perfect day, and we shall rise by degrees into that high position that God intends for his children, to make them gods, to dwell in his presence for ever and ever. Amen.

Orson Pratt 15:241

It is the spirit of truth that reveals the things of the Father and the Son, proceeding from the presence of the Almighty and the very glory in which He is enrobed, which makes Him like unto a consuming fire. If we receive that heavenly gift all are brought into communion with Him; we can understand something concerning Him, that we may pattern after Him until we become like Him; for if we are continually guided by that spirit, eventually we will come back to His presence and be able to enjoy the fullness of His glory.

Charles W. Penrose 23:350
See also 2:342-343; 19:22

13

We Are to Become Sanctified

Wherever the servants of God have gone bearing this message, and the people have received it and obeyed the requirements of the Gospel, they have received the Holy Ghost as a gift from on high; and if they have been led by its light it has increased in them day by day, and they are still going on, their light growing brighter and brighter unto the perfect day. . . .

If the inhabitants of the earth will walk according to the light that God has given them, whether by the spirit that came to them naturally in their birth, or by that higher endowment called the gift of the Holy Ghost, they will receive a still greater degree of power and light, and their pathway will become brighter and brighter even to the perfect day.

Charles W. Penrose 23:352

Becoming Sanctified

The knowledge we now have in our possession is sufficient to guide and direct us step by step, day by day, until we are made perfect before the Lord our Father. If we do not take a course to sanctify the Lord God in our hearts, and attain to perfection, I do not intend to be satisfied with either myself or anyone who comes short of this.

Brigham Young 8:167

I have often told you from this stand, if you cleave to holy, godlike principles, you add more good to your organization, which is made independent in the first place, and the good spirit and influence which come from the Father of lights, and from Jesus Christ, and from the holy angels add good to it.

And when you have been proved, and when you have labored and occupied sufficiently upon that, it will become, in you, what brother Joseph Smith told Elder Taylor, if he would adhere to the Spirit of the Lord strictly, it should become in him, viz., a fountain of revelation. That is true.

After a while the Lord will say to such, "My son, you have been faithful, you have clung to good, and you love righteousness, and hate iniquity, from which you have turned away, now you shall have the blessing of the Holy Spirit to lead you, and be your constant companion, from this time henceforth and forever."

Then the Holy Spirit becomes your property, it is given to you for a profit, and an eternal blessing. It tends to addition, extension, and increase, to immortality and eternal lives.

Brigham Young 2:135

But where division of sentiment, diversity of feeling, and discord exist, the principles of heaven are not there; the principles of peace are not there. Study these principles, and for what purpose? Why, that it may stir up the spirit of peace within you — that the spirit of peace may be, not a casual visitor, but a constant attendant — that he may take up his abode with you; and when an individual takes up his abode with you, then you do not consider him a transient visitor, but there is his home — there is where he lodges, where he stays, where he imparts blessings — if he is a minister of blessings, where he imparts good, if he has any good to impart.

And if you open a door that this Spirit will take up his abode with you, then that fountain which will be opened up will become very plenteous in its supplies; it will become so to you because you welcome the Holy Spirit there, and you study to cultivate within you such a feeling that the Spirit will love to tarry with you day by day; and its book of instructions will be opened to you, so that each succeeding day will give you an increase of knowledge, and you will find yourselves able to comprehend one degree of light and knowledge after another, until your whole soul will be swallowed up in your love for the truth; your affections will be bound up in the truth, for which you will be willing to sacrifice all. . . .

What will this prepare you for? For any contingency that may arise; and you will be contented in the storm and confident of what the result will be. If the storm clouds lour around you, you will be comforted by the sunshine of the Spirit of God; and however dark the clouds that may lour around, you will find that Spirit to be your companion; you will see the sunshine that opens to you the prospect of happiness, of glory, and of eternal life when the clouds shall pass away.

Why will this be the case? Because you have prepared yourselves that the Spirit might be in you, having cultivated it all through your lives. Then you have a devotion to the truth, and the Spirit of truth will tarry with you, and by-and-by you will become fully devoted to the truth; your affections will become pure and holy; and then when you are purified and made holy, you will not depart from the truth, nor go into darkness and apostacy, because the sunlight of truth is within you.

Amasa M. Lyman 5:310

It is our privilege to come near unto our Father, to drink of those streams that flow from the eternal fountain, to have the Holy Ghost in our hearts every day, springing up "like a well of water unto everlasting life."

It is our privilege to walk in the light continually, and have the Holy Ghost to be our constant companion, directing our ways, not only our actions and our doings, but our feelings and our thoughts and our sentiments, that we may become purer and holier, day by day, until we are sanctified and made clean and white and fit to go back into the presence of our Heavenly Father.

Charles W. Penrose 25:47

If we live according to our covenants we will always enjoy the light of truth, and if we live faithful enough we shall enjoy blessings of the Holy Ghost to be our constant companion. In such case no person would turn either to the right hand or the left, in consequence of the motives, the sayings, or the doings of this one or that one; but they would march straight forward in the path that leads to eternal life; and if others stepped out of the way, they would walk straight along.

Brigham Young 10:289

I am not aware that we, as a people, have any policy marked out by which to meet the issues or overcome the annoyances which may be forced upon us, but with those who merit the constant companionship of the Holy Ghost, all will be well.

The sight of the eye, the hearing of the ear, the touch of the hand may each and all be deceived, but the instructions of the spirit are in all things correct. The combined senses may misguide or fail, but he who happily secures the companionship of the Holy Spirit, walks in the ways of life and neither fears, becomes weary nor faints by the wayside.

Christ is the author of human redemption — himself a willing sacrifice — comprehending by his divine nature, the fullness of this great truth, commanded his disciples to tarry at Jerusalem until endowed with power from on high — until He should send the Comforter whose mission it was to show them things to come, bring all things which He had taught to their remembrance and lead them into all truth.

Moses Thatcher 23:196-197

How to Become Sanctified

A. Must Give Yourself Wholly to God

Again, I can charge you with what you will all plead guilty of, if you would confess the truth, viz., you dare not quite give up all your hearts to God, and become sanctified throughout, and be led by the Holy Ghost from morning until evening, and from one year's end to another. I know this is so, and yet few will acknowledge it. I know this feeling is in your hearts, as well as I know the sun shines. . . .

If I were to ask you individually, if you wished to be sanctified throughout, and become as pure and holy as you possibly could live, every person would say yes; yet if the Lord Almighty should give a revelation instructing you to be given wholly up to Him, and to His cause, you would shrink, saying, "I am afraid he will take away some of my darlings." That is the difficulty with the majority of this people. It is for you and I to wage war with that principle until it is overcome in us, then we shall not entail it upon our children.

Brigham Young 2:134

B. Subdue Your Passions

We say we want the Holy Spirit; then let us so live our religion that we may have the Holy Spirit, which will improve our condition continually, making us better and better citizens of the kingdom of God with every degree of gain over ourselves. . . .

If we strive to subdue stormy passions within us, he will assist us in the good work until the Spirit of God is not merely a casual visitor, but a constant dweller within us to increase our store of knowledge, extend our views and make our conceptions of God and truth more as they should be. Let us live in this way and we shall speak kindly of one another and be more charitable to all men.

Amasa M. Lyman 10:86-87

And the fact that we receive this Comforter, the Holy Ghost, is proof that the spirit in warring with the flesh has overcome, and by continuing in this state of victory over our sinful bodies we become the sons and daughters of God, Christ having made us free, and whoever the Son makes free is free indeed.

Brigham Young 18:259

God will talk with His own creation, and if that spirit in man will place itself in a position to listen to the voice of God, what will he say to that spirit, "Control that tabernacle, I gave it to you for a greater exaltation; I gave it to you that after it shall have passed away, it may be resurrected from the grave, and if you subdue its passions, its unholy desires, if you sanctify that tabernacle before Me, then I am bound to bring that tabernacle from the grave and to bring it to the enjoyment of the fullness of My glory, which was the destiny of the spirit when it was first created."

Joseph E. Taylor 23:247

We want the spirit, knowledge, power and principle within us to govern and control our tempers; there is no danger of having too much if we will only control them by the Spirit of the Almighty.

Every intelligent being on the earth is tempered for glory, beauty, excellency and knowledge here, and for immortality and eternal lives in the worlds to come. But every being who attains to this must be sanctified before God and be completely under the control of His Spirit. If I am thus controlled by the Spirit of the Most High I am a king, I am supreme so far as the control of self is concerned. . . .

Brigham Young 13:273

Cast all bitterness out of your own hearts — all anger, wrath, strife, covetousness, and lust, and sanctify the Lord God in your hearts, that you may enjoy the Holy Ghost, and have that Spirit to be your constant companion day by day, to lead you into all truth, and then you will have good doctrine, good feelings, good wives, good children, a good community; and finally, you will be Saints in the fullest sense of the word, but not yet. I believe we shall be Saints, through the grace of God.

Brigham Young 8:33

C. Become One in Your Families

The men who are sitting here this day ought to be, when in the presence of their families, filled with the Holy Ghost, to administer the word of life to them as it is administered in this stand from sabbath to sabbath. When they kneel down in the presence of their wives and children they ought to be inspired by the gift and power of the Holy Ghost, that the husband may be such a man as a good wife will honor, and that the gift and power of God may be upon them continually.

They ought to be one in their families, that the Holy Ghost might descend upon them, and they ought to live so that the wife through prayer may become sanctified, that she may see the necessity of sanctifying herself in the presence of her husband, and in the presence of her children, that they may be one together, in order that the man and the wife may be pure element, suitable to occupy a place in the establishment and formation of the kingdom of God, that they may breathe a pure spirit and impart pure instruction to their children, and their children's children.
  Lorenzo Snow 4:155

D.   Become Pure and Clean

That is the office of the Holy Ghost — to dwell and abide with those who keep the commandments of the Almighty in faith believing. He delights to dwell with such; but he does not delight to dwell in unholy temples. You know that naturally, because there is not one of you, unless you make a practice of being filthy and dirty yourselves, that ever wishes to go into a filthy place. Now, if these are your feelings, for heaven's sake do not ask the Holy Ghost to dwell with you, when you do not pursue a course to cleanse the body, not only internally, but externally, from the crown of the head to the soles of the feet. You know this is what I believe to be sanctification.
  Heber C. Kimball 7:17

I know that it may be said, and with great propriety, "Why, my brother, we cannot be sanctified in one day, we cannot overcome every evil and every passion in one day." That is true, but this holy desire can dwell in the heart of every individual from the time that he or she is convinced that God reigns, that he is establishing his kingdom on the earth, that Jesus is our Savior, that the holy Gospel has presented to us the way of life and salvation, and we believe it and can receive it with our whole hearts.

I say we can have that holy and pure desire from that moment to the end of our lives, and in possessing this we have faith and favor before the Lord, and his grace is with us by the power of his Holy Spirit, and by this we can overcome temptations as we meet them. This is my experience, that is pretty good proof, is it not?
  Brigham Young 16:27

The Effect on the Individual of Being Sanctified

Created by the Almighty, gold, when honestly acquired, becomes a means of ministering to the comfort and convenience of man; but there is that which the Lord bestows upon the honest, obedient and good, of far higher value.

The Holy Ghost, the Comforter, hath the power of peace and bestows salvation upon obedient humanity, regardless of their earthly surroundings. Let us, therefore, secure the Holy Ghost, and in the testimony of the Father and of the Son which He alone bestows, we shall have secured the "pearl of great price," which the world can neither give nor take away.

Let us gain the constant companionship of the Holy Ghost, and the doctrines of the Priesthood will distil upon our minds as the dews of heaven, and the gates that lead to peace and happiness in time and in eternity will, by the power and authority of his keys, stand wide open for us to pass through to exaltation, dominion and glory.

> Moses Thatcher 26:205

That Spirit which we received by being obedient to the Gospel covenant will be our constant guide and companion in sickness and in health; and what is the feeling of that individual who enjoys the sweet and benign influences of the Holy Ghost?

He acknowledges the hand of God in all things, whether in life or in death, in prosperity or in adversity; it matters not what his situation may be, all is right with him. He merely wishes to know what there is for him to do, and he is all alive in "Mormonism."

Such an individual is willing to be taught the simple things of the kingdom, and he will not ridicule "Mormonism" in any respect, neither will he suffer it to be done under his roof, nor upon his possessions, and he is willing to lay down his life for it, and Jesus said, "Greater love has no man than this, that a man lay down his life for his friends."

> Ezra T. Benson 3:62

14

When God
Withdraws the Spirit

Why?

But now having spoken so much about the benefits of this light, and how good it would be to be continually guided and instructed by the spirit of revelation, there is another thing connected with it which we perhaps do not all fully understand.

Supposing a person were thus guided all the time, from waking in the morning until they retired to rest at night; and then when asleep if his dreams were given by the same spirit, and this should be the uninterrupted condition of an individual, I ask, where would be his trials?

This would lead us to ask, is it not absolutely necessary that God should in some measure, withhold even from those who walk before him in purity and integrity, a portion of his Spirit, that they may prove to themselves, their families and neighbors, and to the heavens whether they are full of integrity even in times when they have not so much of the Spirit to guide and influence them? I think that this is really necessary, consequently I do not know that we have any reason to complain of the darkness which occasionally hovers over the mind.

Orson Pratt 15:233

If I am to receive these blessings [to become Gods] I will be an independent character, like those who dwell in eternity. If this is the case, let me pause for a moment and use my own natural philosophy. How can I prove myself the friend of God, who has placed all this glory within my reach, unless His influences are withdrawn from me, to see whether or not I will be His friend?

At the time when you receive the greatest blessings by the manifestations of the power and Spirit of God, immediately the Lord may leave you to yourselves, that you may prove yourselves worthy of this exaltation.

Multitudes, on the right hand and on the left, when this Spirit and power are withdrawn from them, sin into unbelief, and do not know whether there is a God, or not. Ask them, "What did you realize and experience yesterday?" The reply is, "I do not know anything about it. I can see this house, I can see the sun, I can see men and women, but I can say no more." "Do you believe what you believed yesterday?" "I do not know."

Can a man be exalted upon any other principle? When men are left to themselves, it is then they manifest their integrity, by saying and feeling, "I am the friend of God." Do all people realize that? If they did, let me tell you, they would cling fast to their integrity.

When the mind of a righteous man is beclouded by darkness, when he does not know the first thing about the religion he believes in, it is because the vail is dropped so that he may act on the organization of his own individual person, which is calculated to be as independent as the Gods, in the end. When you are fully aware of this, then you are ready to lay down your lives for the cause of God and for His people, if you act on your own integrity and philosophy.

One of the greatest trials that ever came on the Son of God when he was in the flesh, upon that man whom we hold as our Saviour, was when the mob had him in their possession. They spit on him, scourged him, mocked him, and made a wreath of thorns and placed it upon his head (and I will [assure you] that it was so placed on his head as to cause the blood to start) and said to him, "Here is your cross, you poor, worthless scamp, take and carry it on to that hill, for there we are going to nail you to it."

How would you feel in such a time, and at that very hour and moment when this tabernacle suffers, should the Father then withdraw Himself and say, "Now, my son, I will see whether you will prove yourself worthy or not." Did he walk up the hill? He did, and carried the cross until he fainted under it; then they took it and went on, and he submitted patiently to the will of his Father.

Will you submit patiently to the will of your Father in the hour of darkness? Will you say that you are the friends of God? O shame! Many of you will not say so, in the hour of darkness.
Brigham Young 4:199

We should learn our own nature, and live worthy of our being.

When Jesus Christ was left to Himself, in His darkest hour, He faltered not, but overcame. He was ordained to this work. If we should ever be left to ourselves, and the Spirit withdrawn from us, it will be to try the strength of our integrity and faithfulness, to see whether we will walk in His ways even in a dark and cloudy hour.
    Brigham Young 12:174

What Do We Do?

While Lehi was on his way to this country he dreamed that he wandered many hours in darkness; that there was a certain rod of iron, notwithstanding this darkness that seemed to gather around him, on which the old man leaned steadfastly.

So great was the darkness that he was fearful he should lose his way if he let go the rod of iron; but he clung to it, and continued to wander on until, by and by, he was brought out into a large and spacious field, and he also was brought out to a place where it was lighter, and he saw a certain tree which bore very precious fruit. And he went forth and partook of the fruit of this tree, which was the most precious and desirable of any fruit that he had ever tasted; and it seemed to enlighten him and fill him with joy and happiness.

Lehi was a good old man — a man who had been raised up as a great prophet in the midst of Jerusalem. He had prophesied in the midst of all that wickedness which surrounded the Jews; and they sought to take away his life, because of his prophecy. But notwithstanding this gift of prophecy, and the gifts of the Spirit which he enjoyed, the Lord showed him by this dream that there would be seasons of darkness through which he would have to pass, and that even then there was a guide.

If he did not all the time have the Spirit of God upon him to any great extent, there was the word of God, represented by an iron rod, to guide him; and if he would hold fast to that in his hours of darkness and trial, when everything seemed to go against him, and not sever himself therefrom, it would finally bring him where he could partake of the fruit of the precious tree — The Tree of Life. Consequently, I am not so sure, that it is intended for men of God to enjoy all the time a great measure of his Spirit. . . .

But all these great Prophets, Seers and Revelators had to experience their seasons of darkness and trial, and had to show their integrity before God in the midst of the difficulties they had to encounter. Shall the Latter-day Saints despond, then, because they may have seasons of darkness, and may be brought into trials and difficulties? No!

Let us be steadfast, holding fast to the rod of iron — the word of God — and to our honesty, integrity and uprightness, that God may be well pleased with us whether we have much or little of the Spirit. I do not know how we could have many trials, if we were all the time filled with the Spirit and continually having revelations. . . .

What I have said has been with the design to comfort and encourage the Saints, that they may not think, because some are tried this way, and some that way, and some another, that something has befallen them different to what has taken place upon the human family before, and that they are more tried than any other individual that has ever been upon the earth.

Do not think this, Latter-day Saints, but strengthen yourselves in God, and in the hour of your trial call upon him, and he will impart strength and faith to you, light up your understandings, and bring you through victoriously, and your blessings will be still greater than before your temptations came upon you.

Orson Pratt 15:234-237

15

When We Cause the Spirit's Withdrawal

Violating Our Covenants, Sinning

Brother Lyman has well said that it is the Spirit shed abroad upon the Latter-day Saints, bearing witness unto them of the truth — which is the witness of the Holy Ghost of the Father and of the Son — that makes them steadfast and immovable.

They cannot be turned away so long as they enjoy this Spirit; they cannot be turned away from the light of the Gospel and the liberties they enjoy in Christ Jesus; they cannot be converted to Catholicism, nor Methodism, nor any other ism; but if they fall into sin, if they violate their holy covenants, if they grieve the Holy Spirit from them, then they are left in great darkness.

As the Savior said to His disciples: "The light of the body is the eye; if, therefore, thine eye be single, thy whole body shall be full of light. But if thine eye be evil, thy whole body shall be full of darkness. If, therefore, that which is in thee be darkness, how great is that darkness" . . . .

Brother Lyman has well said, also, that when men apostatize from the truths of heaven, and become infidel to the things of God, it is because of sin and transgression; it is because they have given way to evil; it is because they have corrupted their ways, defiled their tabernacles, defiled their spirits, violated their own consciences, or given themselves up to work sin and wickedness.

All this they may have done in the dark, or in secret, and not upon the housetops; but the time cometh when the secrets of all hearts shall be revealed, and every secret thing shall be made known upon the housetops. Then it shall be known and read of men the causes that operated to take away the light and the truth from the hearts of men and left them to go into outer and utter darkness.

None are proof against the attacks of the enemy, against the powers of evil, against the evil devices of the wicked one; none are proof against or safe from the influence and power thereof, without watchfulness and prayer, without so living that the Spirit will have pleasure to abide with them, to be their monitor and protector.

That Spirit will not dwell in unholy temples, it will not continue to dwell with those who violate their own consciences, corrupt their ways, defile their spirits and tabernacles, and defile themselves with their fellow creatures; for God will have a pure people. His Kingdom is holy; His dominions are pure; and no impure thing can inherit the Kingdom of God.

Erastus Snow 25:71, 72

And the Spirit of the Lord will strive, and strive, and strive with the people, till they have sinned away the day of grace. Until then, all are entitled to the light of Christ, for he is the light that lighteth every man who cometh into the world.

Brigham Young 10:296

Forgetting That God and Angels Are Watching Us

Many of us give way to temptation; we falter and get into darkness, and lose the Spirit of the Lord. We forget that God and angels are looking upon us; we forget that the spirits of just men made perfect and our ancient fathers, who are looking forward for the establishment of the kingdom of God upon the earth, are gazing upon us, and that our acts are open to the inspection of all the authorized agencies of the invisible world.

And, forgetting these things sometimes, we act the part of fools, and the Spirit of God is grieved; it withdraws from us, and we are then left to grope our way in the dark.

But if we could live our religion, fear God, be strictly honest, observe his laws and his statutes, and keep his commandments to do them, we should feel very different; we should feel comfortable and happy; our spirits would be peaceful and buoyant; and from day to day, from week to week, and from year to year, our joys would increase.

John Taylor 6:164-165

Neglecting to Pray/Succumbing to Anger

If the Saints neglect to pray, and violate the day that is set apart for the worship of God, they will lose His Spirit. If a man shall suffer himself to be overcome with anger, and curse and swear, taking the name of the Deity in vain, he cannot retain the Holy Spirit.

In short, if a man shall do anything which he knows to be wrong, and repenteth not, he cannot enjoy the Holy Spirit, but will walk in darkness and ultimately deny the faith. Every good and wholesome law we should obey strictly, and do it with a good and honest heart. If we will pursue this course, the Lord Almighty will put hooks in the jaws of our enemies, and lead them whithersoever He will.

Brigham Young 11:134

Practicing Impurity

We know that it is as strict a law of heaven as any other that has been given, that the man who enters into this Church, and practices impurity, will lose the Spirit of God, and, sooner or later, will be opposed to this Work. This is a truth that has been proclaimed almost daily in our hearing, from the time the Church was organized until now. There is no general truth that has been so frequently dwelt upon, and so powerfully enforced upon the minds of this people, as this truth to which I now allude.

We who are connected with this Church, and retain our membership with this people, must be pure in our thoughts, in our words, and in our actions; we must take a course to retain the Spirit of God in our hearts; and if we do not take a course of this kind, the Spirit of God will inevitably leave us, and that light which has illumined our understandings, that joy and peace which have filled our souls and caused us to rejoice exceedingly before the Lord, will depart from us, and we shall be left in a worse condition than we were before we obeyed the Gospel.

George Q. Cannon 11:226

Neglecting Our Duty

Those Elders about to start on their missions will declare before this congregation and before the whole world that they do know, by the power of God, that Joseph Smith is a true Prophet of God, and that this is the work of God; that God has set to his hand to gather Israel: but let them neglect their duty and get into darkness, and they will lose this Spirit and testimony. They do not see this with their natural eyes, for it is spiritually discerned, as all things of God are.

Let them do wrong and lose the Spirit, and by-and-by they apostatize and declare that they do not know "Mormonism" to be true, and think that they never did. How many are there of this class? Brethren, live your religion. As a mischievous child needs constant watching to keep it from falling into the fire, or otherwise injuring itself, so you need watching, warning, teaching, and admonishing all the time; you need to be continually teased to your duty.

Brigham Young 8:177

But do you not see that if the people are asleep, and slothful, and not living up to their privileges, and the Spirit of God begins to flow from the head to the body, that it soon becomes obstructed and dammed up?

Wilford Woodruff 4:191

Following Our Own Opinions and Feelings

Let us nourish that kind Spirit in our bosoms, get light from the pure fountain, and not grieve it away by our unwise and sinful conduct. We frequently do things according to our feelings and opinions, until we in a great degree lose the light of the Spirit which should control, and which would, if we would let it, be a guide to our path and lead us in all that we do and say; and certainly we need it constantly to guide us and to enable us to render ourselves useful, and be the means of doing great good in the kingdom of God.

Daniel H. Wells 9:95

We do not practically comprehend these facts to their full extent, our own selfish interests more or less blind us, we measurably stand in our own light and choke the channel of blessings from heaven, and cannot fully receive from the Giver of all good that blessing, exaltation and glory that he is ever willing to bestow upon all who will acknowledge and love him and worship him in spirit and in truth.

This is a great and important work — one that we do not fully comprehend. When the Spirit of the Lord rests powerfully upon us, we realize it to some extent; but we do not always have that Spirit in such copious measure, and when we are left to ourselves we are weak, frail and liable to err.

This shows to us that we should be more faithful than we have ever been, and that day and night, wherever we are and under whatever circumstances we may be placed, in order to enjoy the Spirit of the Gospel, we must live to God by observing truth, honoring his law, and ever manifest a vigorous determination to accomplish the work he has assigned us.

Joseph F. Smith 11:309

Becoming Too Concerned over Worldly Cares

High Priests, Seventies, and ye Elders of Israel, are you this day prepared with wisdom and power to officiate for the living and the dead, and to lay a pure and holy foundation through your wives and children, that salvation may go forth to the rising generations; or have you neglected qualifying yourselves in your holy callings, and let the cares of the world occupy your entire thoughts and attention, and your minds become dull, your spiritual armor rusty and but little room found in you for the Holy Ghost to abide?

Brethren, your eye should be single to the glory of God, to hearkening to the counsel of brother Brigham, and to the building up of Zion, then your bodies would be filled with spirit, and your understandings with light, and your hearts with joy, and your souls would be quickened into eternal life with the power of the Holy Ghost, you would then become the depositories of that wisdom and knowledge which would qualify you to be saviors unto your brethren and your posterity.

It is the case with many in this community that instead of preparing themselves for positions in the eternal world, they have been satisfied with the cares of this life, and attending to those things which have been for the comfort of themselves and their wives and children; they have been satisfied in exercising themselves in this small way of ambition.

Lorenzo Snow 4:154-155

16

Results of Repelling the Spirit

Fault-finding/Giving Way to the Devil

Now, if we yield obedience to God and to the spirits that dwell within us, then will our light become like that of the just that shineth brighter and brighter unto the perfect day; but if we do not yield an obedience to the law and word and order of the Church and Kingdom of God upon the earth, the light that is within us will become darkness, and then, as it is said, how great is that darkness!

We see sometimes men of that character. They are occasionally referred to as cranks, or, as the Germans use that term, sick. They lose the light, spirit and power of God, and they do not comprehend the order of the Church and Kingdom of God, nor do they place themselves in the way to obtain a knowledge of these things.

The first thing they begin to do is to try to pervert the order of God, and to find fault with their brethren in the Holy Priesthood — with their Bishops, with their Bishop's Counselors, with the High Council, perhaps with Presidents of Stakes, as the case may be, or with the Apostles, or with the First Presidency; no matter which, or how, or when, or where.

Now, if these men were walking in the light as God is the light they would have fellowship one, with another, and the blood of Christ would cleanse them from all sin; but when they begin to murmur and complain, to find fault and to give way to improper influences, they give place to the devil, and he takes possession just as fast and as far as he can, and forces upon them feelings, ideas and principles that are at variance with the law and order, and word and will of God.

John Taylor 26:130-131

Experiencing Darkness

The Savior constantly exhorted His disciples to watch and pray, lest they should fall into temptation, and cautioned them that they who once put their hands to the plow and looked back, or turned away, were not fit for the kingdom of heaven, but that they who endured unto the end, the same should have eternal life.

He warned them against falling into darkness, and, as I have already quoted, He assured them that the light that was in them might become darkness, and if it did, how great should be that darkness.

Erastus Snow 25:71

Salvation should be the uppermost thing with us, and you will find if we ever seek to do something else besides carrying out the dictates of the Holy Spirit, we will get into the fog and into darkness and trouble, and we shall be ignorant of the way we are pursuing. Every day that we live we need the power of the Lord — the power of His Holy Spirit and the strength of the Priesthood to be with us that we may know what to do.

And if we will so live before the Lord, the Spirit will reveal to us every day what our duties are: I do not care what it is we are engaged in, we should first find out the will of the Lord and then do it, and then our work will be well done and acceptable before the Lord, but if we take a course against light and against the Spirit of God, we will find it an unprofitable road to travel.

Wilford Woodruff 4:229-230

When men have the privilege of hearing the plan of salvation from the mouth of an inspired servant of God, and they reject it, I will promise them that if they have ever possessed any portion of the Holy Spirit, it will depart from them and sevenfold more darkness will ensue to the mind of that person than is the lot of all to suffer in a state of nature, unenlightened by the inspiring rays of the Holy Spirit.

Brigham Young 10:323

In the Spirit of the Lord, there is peace, there is joy, there is light, there is truth, there is hope, and there is faith. Without that Spirit all is darkness, all is wretchedness, and all is shut up and closed as it were to the human mind; and future hope, or hope of future blessings and exaltation, is cut off.

Orson Pratt 8:306

Meeting Difficulties

When the Spirit of the Lord influences any man, especially the true and faithful Saint, it fills him with joy and peace, and makes him humble in the performance of duties. The Spirit of the Lord carries with it its own reward. A person deprived of this influence meets with difficulties upon every hand. It is only by being obedient and submitting to the counsel of God in all things, that we can fully enjoy that good Spirit.

> Daniel H. Wells 9:94

May Still Be Taught by Spirit Occasionally

The words of eternal life, the holy Priesthood of the Son of God, with its keys, powers, and blessings, are committed to us. If they and the God who gave them are honoured by this people, great peace and joy are ours, through the Holy Spirit of this Gospel. Great peace have they who love the law of the Lord and abide in his commandments. . . .

If persons reach a period when the Spirit of truth ceases to reflect upon their understandings, then they know nothing of the commandments of the Lord, but follow the lusts of the flesh and of the mind, and are bound to perdition.

So long as persons are in a position that it is possible for them to return to the Lord, after having once received the love of Christ — after having once been enlightened by his Spirit, there will be times when they will be taught whether they are walking in the truth or not.

> Brigham Young 8:121-122

Losing Guidance

When a man revolts against the work of God and against the counsels of his servants, and will not be subject to the Holy Ghost which dwells in him, he commits treason against God, and against his authority on the earth, and neither the Father, nor the Son, nor the Holy Ghost will take up their abode with such a man, and he may bid farewell to the guidance of good angels.

> Heber C. Kimball 11:145

Living Hard Life

How is it with you who do not enjoy the spirit of your religion? It is a hard life for you to live; and you had better, from this day, take a course to enjoy the Spirit of the Lord; then you will be numbered with the wise.

> Brigham Young 8:198

——— 17 ———

Living by the Spirit

And without that Spirit no person can expect to enjoy any great degree of happiness in this life or in that which is to come. It is contrary to the nature of happiness for us to undertake to enjoy ourselves independent of the approbation of Heaven, and independent of the Holy Spirit which the Almighty pours out upon those who are honest and upright before him.

There is no happiness in anything else; there is no place worthy of being called a place of happiness only in the enjoyment of the favor of God and of his Holy Spirit. And those persons are truly blessed who have the greatest share of that Spirit abiding with them; and when that Spirit withdraws from the hearts of mankind, they are truly cursed.

In the Spirit of the Lord there is peace, there is joy, there is light, there is truth, there is hope, and there is faith. Without that Spirit all is darkness, all is wretchedness, and all is shut up and closed as it were to the human mind, and future hope, or hope of future blessings and exaltation, is cut off.

Orson Pratt 8:306

And it is also the privilege of the whole people who are called Israel to obtain the revelations of the Holy Spirit to guide them in every duty in life. Whatever position a man may stand in, it is his privilege, as a Saint of God, to enjoy this blessing; and a man who understands himself will not move without the operations of that Spirit to lead him.

Wilford Woodruff 5:85

I have never asked but one thing of the Latter-day Saints, and that is for them to serve the Lord our God with an undivided heart. One says, "I knew brother Joseph, but I do not know much about brother Brigham." I do not care for this; the question with me is this, do you know Jesus and the Holy Spirit?

I do not care if you never hear any more about brother Brigham, so far as my personal feelings are concerned, if you will only live under the influence of that Spirit which comes from God.

Brigham Young 10:310

To know that we possess the gift of the Holy Spirit — that is, the right to claim the aid and assistance of the Spirit of God to direct us in our labors and course in life, is far greater than the wealth and the honors of this world.

Joseph F. Smith 25:56

It is through the united faith of the people of God — through that confidence which they have in the Being whom they worship, that he, for their edification and benefit, will grant his Spirit unto his humble and faithful Saints.

But we oftentimes deprive ourselves of the blessings and enjoyments which we might receive, through the darkness of our minds, through our selfishness, through our neglect of keeping the commandments of God, through our disobedience, and through the abundance of cares and perplexities with which we have to contend in this mortal existence. All these things have a tendency, more or less, to darken the understanding and drive away from the heart that peaceable Spirit which whispers peace to the minds of the sons and daughters of God.

I often reflect upon this subject much, and inquire in my own mind, and try to search out some of the causes of our being so far beneath the privileges which are guaranteed to us in the Gospel of Jesus Christ. It is not because the promises of God have failed. It is not because we are not worshipping the same Being whom the Saints worshipped in ancient days. It is not because there are insurmountable obstacles in our way; but the cause lies in our own selves. We are the individuals that shut out this light of heaven — this light of truth that would otherwise shine upon our understandings.

Orson Pratt 7:308

When they have once believed in Jesus Christ and have been baptized for the remission of their sins, they can call upon God in all confidence and he is more willing to give his Holy Spirit unto them than earthly parents are to give good gifts unto their children, and you know how willing they are to do that, for they like to see their children joyful and happy. So it is with our Heavenly Father. He likes to see his children who have repented and obeyed his Gospel joyful and happy, and he is willing to give good gifts unto them; but he never can to those who do not keep his commandments. They may pray until they are grey-headed and they are about to fall into their graves and their sins would not be pardoned.

Orson Pratt 14:178